DENNIS DAWSON ELLIOTT

ARMAGEDDON
of a
DIFFERENT ORDER

Wake Up, America

ARMAGEDDON OF A DIFFERENT ORDER
WAKE UP, AMERICA

iUniverse books may be ordered through booksellers or by contacting:

iUniverse
1663 Liberty Drive
Bloomington, IN 47403
www.iuniverse.com
1-800-Authors (1-800-288-4677)

Because of the dynamic nature of the Internet, any web addresses or links contained in this book may have changed since publication and may no longer be valid. The views expressed in this work are solely those of the author and do not necessarily reflect the views of the publisher, and the publisher hereby disclaims any responsibility for them.

Any people depicted in stock imagery provided by Getty Images are models, and such images are being used for illustrative purposes only. Certain stock imagery © Getty Images.

ISBN: 978-1-5320-6199-8 (sc)
ISBN: 978-1-5320-6201-8 (hc)
ISBN: 978-1-5320-6200-1 (e)

Library of Congress Control Number: 2018914134

Print information available on the last page.

iUniverse rev. date: 12/21/2018

To my family, friends, and colleagues, and to all those who appreciate the principles, ethics, truth, and integrity necessary for American democracy to continue to flourish

CONTENTS

INTRODUCTION

The time to reflect on the legacy of a president often comes once that individual is no longer in office. Years later, as more study of the president's time in office is analyzed with attention to achievements and failures, comparisons are made to other presidents.

Presently, the country faces a dysfunctional administration and president, both of which exhibit narcissistic flair, missteps, misstatements, insults, and actions that do not reflect the country's heritage or current needs.

In the pages that follow, the reader should not assume partisan bias on my part. Instead, my approach was to examine how Donald Trump managed to become the Republican Party's nominee and to assess his qualifications and shortcomings and the turmoil that has ensued before and since his election. This book is a challenge to all Americans to stand up and support their country in reasonable, responsible, and ethical ways regardless of personal ideological leanings.

I will pose questions readers can answer with their own assessments of facts and personal bias; the most important questions I ask are these: Is this president acting in ways that command respect for the country and its democracy? Does he have the ability to bring the country together? We can only look forward, not back.

The overriding perspective I employed in writing this book came from my education as a journalism major, a field in which I earned undergraduate and graduate degrees, from a communications career in the business sector, and from my later position as a journalism faculty member at Indiana University.

My teaching concentrations were in the areas of public relations principles, public relations planning and research, social media strategy, crisis management, and media ethics. Case studies were a valuable tool for focusing student learning, and it is not coincidental that a common platform for these studies included the First Amendment, ethical decision-making, and the metrics of personal integrity and honesty.

In a short time, the country began to see that the Trump presidency would be punctuated by behaviors and actions not considered normal for a leader of our country. What some considered showmanship and boisterous rhetoric during the primaries and the election campaign ultimately found their way into the Oval Office.

With great frequency, Trump continued to criticize his presidential election opponent and the previous administration even after taking office. His repetitive banter had little substance. His reliance on Twitter as his means of speaking loudly surfaced in his ongoing and narcissistic need to boast, but he offered little or no substantiation for his claims.

Trump has maintained the support of his base, but the majority of Americans, when polled, report their disapproval of Trump's governing record and abilities.[1] He willingly professes success in some areas, yet facts confirm that the root of what he takes credit for actually began prior to his taking office. He has made nepotistic appointments to his staff that have generated more controversy than meaningful contributions to the country's governance.

He has alienated long-standing allies and criticized other world leaders while complimenting enemies and dictators. He has overwhelmingly taken an "unscramble the egg" approach by showing little regard for the meaning or success of programs and policies in place when he took office. The revolving door for those leaving and joining the Trump administration is in a constant state of spin.

As time passes and the special counsel investigation continues, more questions arise that require answers, more players are under the microscope, and the administration's paranoia and perhaps fear are increasing. Perhaps most disturbing is that true and responsible governing has taken a back seat to the president's idiosyncrasies and their negative and damaging impact on the country.

It would be relatively easy to list the missteps of this presidency thus far. Perhaps the larger concern should be about allowing this president to drown all that is right about our country and its institutions of democracy while stifling the true needs of the US and at the same time challenging the positive world order with the country's strongest allies. His need to aggrandize himself by thinking he can enhance his power, position, and reputation through outrageous behavior is highly concerning.

There is little evidence thus far that he will come to understand that the office of the presidency is not above the law and that he cannot run roughshod over the Constitution in general and the First Amendment in particular.

Living for personal gain and headlines while entertaining himself allows the president to project a disheartening image to the world. He exists in a Trump realm steered by his need to be viewed as great and powerful. He is missing the obvious in many ways in that very experienced world leaders with their own agendas will reflect on his actions and at some point will act on their observations in ways that may be detrimental to the United States. The most notable player in this game is Russian president Vladimir Putin, particularly when Trump's view of the former KGB agent is so positive for reasons unclear to most.

Trump must believe only he can recognize truth, a truth he embraces that satisfies his personal needs. The statements emanating from Trump and those around him portray truth as a moving and false target and perhaps even identify it as an objective that has become unimportant. Trump's version of truth appears in the form of his latest tweet devoid of supporting facts. He describes the simplest reporting of his words and his changes of position on issues as fake while he looks for personal and political cover. While his staff incredibly struggles to support his statements, he focuses on undermining the media and freedom of the press by fostering a morass of attacks and personal threats delivered in person and through Twitter.

To his dismay, his words and actions create more questions. He becomes frustrated, ignores advice, and responds with false claims. If his objective is to create controversy and encourage coverage of his image across the media landscape, he has been unquestionably successful. He has repeatedly experienced the reality that he is unable to manipulate Congress and others in the ways that may have worked in the creation of his real estate kingdom. He has shown that he does not understand the processes and relationships between the branches of government outlined in the Constitution, and he most assuredly ignores the concept of the separation of powers.

Americans and those around the world who look to the United States as a leader for policies that represent clear thought and direction have been disappointed by Trump and his haphazard approach to all things.[2] He has sought to exercise personal power by turning the government on its head. He has suffocated significant progress on many fronts. Because of his and his party's leaders' lack of true legislative guidance, partisan politics have thwarted the development of solutions to pending problems.

He has an unchallenged ability to make assertions and in the same setting seconds later to repeat portions of his pronouncements with his patented "We'll have to see" as a cover so he won't be pinned down. In most instances, he actually says little of value as through his statements the credibility bar is lowered.

> *The supreme quality for leadership is unquestionably integrity. Without it, no real success is possible, whether it is on a section gang, a football field, in an army, or in office.*
>
> —Dwight D. Eisenhower

A true leader would recognize that a personal, narrow-minded agenda has little chance of ever being 100 percent achievable. Leaders put others before themselves; they negotiate rather than manipulate. They distinguish between choosing subordinates based on experience and qualification rather than choosing those easily directed and controlled. Leaders encourage informed reason and insights as approaches to challenges. Trump operates in direct opposition to these leadership characteristics. The country is firmly mired in multiple crises of growing proportions, some of which he created, and these are coupled with his personal problems that seem to proliferate wildly. The potential peril Trump presents for our country and the world is epic and alarming.

In a 2017 address to a TED conference, Pope Francis clearly identified what this president was missing—humility.

> Allow me to say it loud and clear: the more powerful you are, the more your actions will have an impact

on people, the more responsible you are to act humbly. If you don't, your power will ruin you, and you will ruin the other.[3]

The pope offered sage advice.

This president displays malevolence and selfishness in ways that point only to the destruction of human rights and principles of the United States and most assuredly point away from what is good and responsible. He seemingly worships conflict but to no productive end. He has personally attacked significant legislative accomplishments and policies of prior administrations regardless of their party affiliations. He has damaged important global relationships with allies while complimenting multiple dictators across the world who pose threats in one form or another to many. He has made dreadful personnel decisions in an attempt to build his administration's organizational chart. Like a dog with a bone, even in the face of information and facts counter to his opinion, he won't let go of his inflammatory rhetoric, because his jargon incites a vocal cohort of his supporters who respond favorably to his dictatorial bellowing.

He oversimplifies his abilities and accomplishments, most of which have yet to be proven successful. Prior to his meeting with Kim Jong-un of North Korea, he declared that Kim was a fine man whom his people loved, and on the same day of the meeting, he said that if he found he was wrong about Kim, "I'll find some kind of an excuse."[4] This logic is sophomoric; he continues to have little understanding of the power of words and how his declarations have potential negative implications with multiple audiences. He demonstrated that during an overseas trip to attend a NATO meeting, a meeting with UK prime minister Theresa May, and his "summit" meeting with Putin.

At the NATO meeting, he showed his lack of knowledge or

understanding of Article 5,[5] or he was just willing to throw away any confidence European allies might have in his role as president of the US. Article 5 has been invoked only once in NATO's nearly seventy-year history, and that was to support the US after the 9/11 attacks. His remarks blasted NATO member nations on a variety of points particularly concerning financial commitments, and then he later attempted to make nice by agreeing to strengthen the alliance against Russia and stating he believed in NATO.

He later claimed to have secured commitments for billions of dollars from NATO members, which of course remains to be confirmed. The 2 percent of GDP commitment for countries was agreed to in 2014, and the goal was for that level to be reached by 2024, a fact glossed over, unstated, by Trump.

Then it was on to the UK, where he insulted the prime minister regarding her Brexit plan: "I would have done it much differently. I actually told Theresa May how to do it, but she didn't listen to me."[6] He has yet to prove he is intelligently capable of governing in the US, but he tells other countries they are doing it wrong.

Next came his highly controversial private meeting with Putin. As of this writing, no information has authoritatively come out about his private meeting and any concessions, agreements, or promises made. Following this meeting with Putin, Trump clearly found the opportunity to get in his own way as again words failed him particularly as he tried to make himself more authoritative than to date he has shown he can be.

At a joint press conference broadcast worldwide, Trump's needy persona once again raised its head. An Associated Press reporter asked Trump,

> President Putin denied having anything to do with the election interference in 2016. Every US intelligence agency has concluded that Russia did.

My first question for you, sir is, who do you believe? My second question is: would you now, with the whole world watching, tell President Putin, would you denounce what happened in 2016 and would you want him to never do it again?[7]

In his typical approach, Trump offered a deflection about the functioning of the FBI and its failure to "not take the server." More to the point, he stated that Director of National Intelligence Dan Coats said Russia was involved in the election, but then he added, "I have President Putin. He just said it's not Russia. I will say this: I don't see any reason why it would be … I will tell you that President Putin was extremely strong and powerful in his denial today." Again, he undermined the US intelligence agencies that have compiled significant proof of Russia's meddling in the election.

The reaction from many quarters in the US, including many Republicans and members of his cabinet, was harshly negative. Realizing the continuing fallout from his statements, the next day, he made an attempt at clarification.

In a key sentence in my remarks, I said the word "would" instead of "wouldn't." The sentence should have been, "I don't see any reason why it wouldn't be Russia." Sort of a double negative. So you can put that in, and I think that probably clarifies things pretty good by itself.[8]

So Putin said there was no Russia meddling. Intelligence agencies said the opposite. Trump then said he didn't see why Russia would have been involved. Then Trump later "corrected" his statement to read that he didn't see any reason why it wouldn't be Russia (as opposed to someone else?). So there you have it.

Step 1: He believes Putin and casts doubt on our intelligence agencies. This according to Trump logic must be true because Putin was strong and powerful. Step 2: he contradicts his own intelligence agencies' opinions. Step 3: he then asks why wouldn't it be Russia. Doesn't his own clarification imply Russia involvement (i.e., I don't believe what my friend Putin told me)? Confusion reigns with Trumpspeak, and Putin may have been heard laughing in Moscow.

From the outset of his presidency, Trump has showcased his ethnic biases through racist remarks. He vocally embraced the actions and qualities of white supremacists in Charlottesville ("fine people on both sides") that precipitated significant negative response across the country, but he doesn't seem to care. He focuses so hard on winning that he continues to bang his drum long after the music has ended.

> *He who passively accepts evil is as much involved in it as he who helps to perpetuate it. He who accepts evil without protesting against it is really cooperating with it.*[9]

—Martin Luther King Jr.

Trump represents Armageddon[10] of a different order and one just as worrisome as the biblical description. Trump's Armageddon is not just something that will occur in the future; it is all around him and the world now. Armageddon is not a foreign policy,[11] but neither do continual, uninformed, egotistical threats constitute policy. The consequences of the Trump presidency, however long it may last, is certain to play out as a downward spiral of lost opportunity for our country facilitated by Trump's comments and actions. Only truth and integrity can overcome the damage already done and block further desecration of the principles on which our country was established. Unfortunately, both of these qualities are easily questioned as the Trump presidency is examined.

Time to wake up, America.

CHAPTER 1

ACCIDENTS DO HAPPEN

With all the power that a President has, the most important thing to bear in mind is this: You must not give power to a man unless, above everything else, he has character. Character is the most important qualification the President of the United States can have.[12]

—President Richard Nixon

It is reasonable to assume that those who run for the office of president will have features in common with all previous presidents and candidates. These include an energetic drive to serve their country, experience in government, knowledge of the concept of checks and balances, a belief they have reasonable and supportable solutions for pressing issues, and a history of ethical behavior, honesty, integrity, character, and intelligence to meet the unknown in a controlled and informed manner. All these features align well with the difficult challenges of the office, and individuals pursuing it should have such attributes that qualify them for it. In human resources terminology, they should be a good fit for the job.

Those interested in the presidency should have the experience and knowledge required to generate informed opinions about any number of issues facing the country. But of critical importance is that they also understand the role of the president, the limitations of the office, and the Constitution. They should accept the need for compromise rather than accepting the stagnation that results from injecting bias and misdirection into the legislative branch. Those who are not objective and conscious of their strengths and weaknesses, are unwilling to listen to others' insights, or are inclined to blame others rather than accepting responsibility for their past failures will have others questioning whether they are good fits for the position.[13]

Donald Trump announced his candidacy in this way: "Sadly, the American dream is dead. But if I get elected president, I will bring it back bigger and better and stronger than ever before."[14] Since his announcement in 2015, Trump has shown he does not have the openness or vulnerability, if you will, that invites the necessary cooperation and compromise that might make his statement a reality. His highly visible and jumbled approach toward any topic, issue, or challenge instead gives rise to real concern that the country will deteriorate to a worsened state, certainly not "better and stronger than ever before." Empty, repetitive claims with no follow-through precipitate a scarcity of positive results and many broken promises.

Past behavior is universally considered a predictor of future behavior and subsequent consequences. Consider Trump's history in the courts. At the time of his nomination for the presidency, Trump had been named in over 3,500 lawsuits, including personal defamation suits, real estate misdeeds, and suits originating from his casino pursuits.[15] Since his inauguration, Trump has been named in over 100 suits.[16] The New York attorney general filed a suit against the Donald J. Trump Foundation, Trump himself, and his three eldest children, alleging "persistently illegal conduct" by the president's personal charity. Trump has most recently agreed to dissolve the Foundation, but the investigation of the Trump family will continue..[17]

Trump is not the first sitting president to be sued, but lawsuits seem to be a way of life for him, some sort of badge of honor. Dragging out resolution in the courts and outspending those who have sought to seek remuneration in some form seems to have been his normative approach in the hope of settlements at significantly reduced levels or having suits dropped.

Trump blames the media for everything negative about him, his staff, his actions, and so on when in reality, the media report his own words; he then claims this is fake news. Americans should be thankful for responsible watchdog journalism because without the free press, they would be tempted to accept everything Trump and his equally controversial cronies and family members say as truth. The concept of a free press as a watchdog will not dissipate as Trump continues to accuse and complain rather than take responsibility. The dangers of electing Trump voiced by many during the Republican primaries and most notably by Jeb Bush predicting Trump would be a "chaos president"[18] were prophetic and even more disturbing than predicted.

How did the country arrive at a point where a governmentally inexperienced individual gained his party's nomination for the presidency and then won the election? The answer to this question does not need to focus on who his opponent was, history, or an intellectual determination. Sixteen other Republicans sought the party's nomination; was none superior to Trump? Republicans may have been offended with the previous administration, but was Trump the best they could do? Was anyone watching what was happening? Did anyone consider what the consequences might have been? Were Republicans looking to Trump to be the great white hope and fund the party's treasury? Until actual voting began, it was widely assumed that Trump's opponent would win.

Did voters ask themselves if Trump's questionable behavior during the debates with his election opponent that featured his boasts, sexist and racist remarks, and petty, visible, narcissistic needs was what the country deserved in its president? Did anyone question whether Trump had the attributes desirable in a president? Did his supporters believe Trump was the guy to embrace change for them, or did they truly not evaluate what he was bringing to the office and the country? Will his base of supporters awaken one day and ask themselves, "What have we done?" Thus far, Trump's base remains steadfast.

If evangelicals were waiting for an answer to their prayers for a president who would fulfill all their wants, needs, and dreams, was Trump really their messiah? Thus far, he has been shown to be more of an Antichrist in terms of his policies as difficult as they are to delineate. What his policies may be are yet to be identified as most everything he addresses becomes moving targets—hard to nail down or accomplish. Trump has shown that he is a reactionary and an autocrat who gives little thought to how his words affect everyone in the world. Shouted expressions at rallies can encourage rage and even violence, but how do they create positive results? Instead, the country and the world are subjected to unsubstantiated ramblings, confusing and error-filled Twitter posts, attacks on individual Americans and others, and frequent changes of position even when he frequently lacks clear understanding of what he is suggesting. Consider his numerous predispositions to repetitively disrespect women, his determination to tear down our democracy's institutions, and his challenging freedom of the press with his fake news claims based on broad exaggerations. It is difficult to view Trump as someone with the ability to make America great again as he continuously drags the country down.

During the debates and his dreadfully informal, wandering, and threatening campaign, Trump was blatantly unconventional in his approach. His rallies were more like tent revivals with Trump the preacher pontificating about whatever came to his mind. His stream-of-consciousness rhetoric precipitated many opportunities for the media to ask him or his spokespersons confirmatory questions, but the responses rarely added any clarity. Instead, he criticized the media for asking any questions at all.

Responsible reporters and media outlets have worked diligently to understand and report Trump's positions and provide a degree of interpretation and insight for the public, but any fact-checking of his statements invariably put them at odds with Trump when his statements were debunked. The result was often Trump's repetitive fake news claims due to his being routinely caught in errors of fact and in making false claims. Trump was being challenged in a responsible manner, but his reaction was to lash out and tweet critical generalizations about what he called the fake media. It became clear that challenging the soothsayer of the Republican Party was unacceptable to him; his only recourse was to criticize the media, which in a rational setting could have been his ally. In spite of the ongoing pattern presented, Trump subsequently went unopposed into his party's 2016 nominating convention in Cleveland.

Without clear insight about how Trump attempts to improve an unmistakable void in facts regarding the country, its needs, and a responsible global perspective, it's obvious that he does at least read headlines. He apparently prefers to watch television as a basis for his next tweet, particularly Fox News, and at times, he uses this source's actual words. This is how he spends what the White House communications staff has termed his "executive time."

> *Facts are stubborn things and whatever may be our wishes, our inclinations or the dictates of our passion, they cannot alter the state of facts and evidence.*[19]

—John Adams

These words from John Adams, a distinguished and significant contributor to the formation of our country, could serve as a valuable guide for Trump and his staff. Trump does indeed *wish* many things; his *inclination* that he is the world's greatest authority on any topic, and he exhibits *passion* in many forms, but exploring the latter is a book in itself. Suffice it to say that Trump doesn't know or care about what he doesn't know. This is evident with the tweets and extreme statements he makes, but none of his traits can change *facts and evidence.*

His staff tries to diffuse, deflect, and otherwise stonewall authentic inquiries and questions about his statements and positions. Many of them have learned from their leader not to let facts get in the way. Perhaps Trump needs to reflect on the possibility that continual deflection of informational needs is just another way of exercising one of his favorite accusations about others. Instead, lying to and cajoling all those around him to walk away from truth—facts and evidence—is the path they are encouraged to take.

> There have been three memorable American presidents, the story goes. President George Washington could never tell a lie. President Richard Nixon could never tell the truth. And President Donald Trump cannot tell the difference.[20]

Perhaps Trump can't recognize the difference and leading with truth is not important to him.

Trump has boasted on multiple occasions, "I was never in politics until two years ago." Can he appreciate the definition of politics? The Merriam-Webster dictionary defines politics as *the art or science concerned with winning and holding control over a government*. Trump is not artful in any sense of the word, and science—for example, climate change—obviously eludes him. Further, he can't control something that he quite obviously doesn't understand. During the primaries and his campaign, he repeatedly stated that he was a winner, that his administration would win, win, and win, and that he would win so often that Americans would become tired of winning.[21]

But Trump has shown that he can't hit any bull's-eye while relying on an empty quiver. Holding control over government is where once again his knowledge, skills, and acumen disappear. Whatever he perceives his legislative agenda to be—which he routinely has difficulty talking about—his ability to achieve it is lacking in spite of his egotistical desire to control. Trump touted his business experience as a benefit for the presidency, but that experience was built on giving orders and others doing the work for success or failure. Thus far, his business experience has been shown to be something far less than effective as president because his directions are fragmented and those who could help he alienates or fires or they resign because of the culture he has created.

Trump broke all the rules when it came to his campaign, and many of those who supported him constituted a class rebellion of sorts. His rhetoric was and is difficult to follow, but it didn't seem to matter as long as his statements attempted to address immigration, gun rights, the environment, antimedia, pro-abortion, and Clinton emails. His exaggerated approach successfully worked his rally crowds into a frenzy as his bully persona came through loud and clear (e.g., "Lock her up!"). His routine response to anyone in the crowd protesting what he was saying or what he represented was condescending, derogatory, and occasionally encouraged a violent response from his audience. There was even a point following a stop in North Carolina where the local sheriff was considering charges of inciting a riot against Trump.

In describing a protester in Birmingham, Alabama, Trump said, "Maybe he should have been roughed up, because it was absolutely disgusting what he was doing."[22]

About a protestor at a Las Vegas rally in 2016, "I love the old days—you know what they used to do to guys like that when they were in a place like this? They'd be carried out on a stretcher, folks ... I'd like to punch him in the face."[23]

At a stop in Cedar Rapids, Iowa, he told the crowd there might be tomato-throwing protesters, and he urged his audience to "knock the crap out of' 'em" if anyone should try. "I promise you, I will pay the legal fees," he added.[24]

The truly disturbing part about such comments, sometimes accompanied by expletives, is that they came from a candidate for the presidency, and since he became president, he has demonstrated the crude and proud side of his self-image. He continues to show traits that are more than unbecoming for a president, and as the country was looking to its future, people in attendance at these rallies were applauding and shouting their support. They were willing to get behind such coarse and unrefined behavior if not actually encourage it.

Then there is Trump's presence on social media. President Obama's campaign, particularly in 2008, demonstrated that these platforms were highly effective in communicating facts and responding to voter interests and questions. Are Trump's Twitter comments just another way to create controversy, perpetuate falsehoods, and deflect? His tweets demonstrate that Trump is all atwitter most of the time; they are broad-brush actions and histrionics in an attempt to degrade the previous president and his policies and actions in a cheap and easy way. However, presenting informed alternatives that require Congress to act, approve, and so on don't surface as threats routinely do. The Constitution does not provide limitless authority and veto power that can't be challenged. Hopefully, very soon, accountability will rule, not Trump's desire to dictate. He should be all atwitter.

His boasts can rarely be substantiated or applied in the real world of the presidency. Inexperienced members of his staff with little knowledge of the world community can't help him. His party's majority position and the well-being of the country are in play. Trump's personal history of business manipulation will not help him succeed as the leader of our country. He should be exceedingly all atwitter.

The country may not have been perfect in every way prior to the election according to Trump's standards, but thus far, he has done little to fulfill his promise of making it great again. Is perfection really an achievable objective, or is working toward progress and learning by inviting informed alternatives along the way more reasonable? Trump speaks (shouts) at every opportunity, distorts facts, and threatens all in his path at home and abroad. If this is his interpretation of what then vice president Teddy Roosevelt's famous big-stick speech was about, he couldn't be more wrong. Roosevelt stated in his speech at the Minnesota State Fair in 1901, "If a man continually blusters, if he lacks civility, a big stick will not save him from trouble; and neither will speaking softly avail, if back of the softness there does not lie strength, power." However, Trump threatened fire and fury if North Korea didn't denuclearize, for example. Hardly soft diplomacy at work. He has entered a world-stage arena, him against everyone else it appears, with little knowledge and even less personal capacity to negotiate on behalf of the United States. His opponents have easily discovered his adoration need, and some may be planning to use this need to their advantage. History will determine if Trump's threats are the new weapons for achieving peace or simply exhibitions of his bully nature.

In characterizing Trump's election victory, Senator Bernie Sanders offered this interpretation.

> Donald Trump tapped into the anger of a declining middle class that is sick and tired of establishment economics, establishment politics and the establishment media. People are tired of working longer hours for lower wages, of seeing decent paying jobs go to China and other low-wage countries, of billionaires not paying any federal income taxes and of not being able to afford a college education for their kids - all while the very rich become much richer. To the degree that Mr. Trump is serious about pursuing policies that improve the lives of working families in this country, I and other progressives are prepared to work with him. To the degree that he pursues racist, sexist, xenophobic and anti-environment policies, we will vigorously oppose him.[25]

Sanders provided this assessment the day after the election. What the country and Sanders have observed since is that Trump has been unable to sustain his boisterous promises with real results and that his broad overall talking points failed miserably. He talks, contradicts himself, talks, changes his position, talks, and tweets some more. He has given little substantive direction to some cabinet members but rather consistently indicts them in public for not reading his mind or for disagreeing with him. He has not presented Congress with detailed plans but instead has pursued a confused path of repetitive, empty tweets on most every topic, including health care, tax reform, and immigration.

> If a new HealthCare Bill is not approved quickly, BAILOUTS for Insurance Companies and BAILOUTS for Members of Congress will end very soon![26]

> Big day for HealthCare. After 7 years of talking, we will soon see whether or not Republicans are willing to step up to the plate![27]

> Mitch, get back to work and put Repeal & Replace, Tax Reform & Cuts and a great Infrastructure Bill on my desk for signing. You can do it![28]

> We don't want what is happening with immigration in Europe to happen with us![29]

If Trump were a magician, his audience would be leaving the room as he reveals no magic behind his tricks. In his case, the tricks he plays for the country and the world only continue to show that hyperbole and chest pounding fail miserably at contributing to any success and fool no one.

There are more questions about this "accidental" president, but many of those answers are difficult to find. Trump's election represents an accident for the country as he based his campaigning on the sound bite of the day, disregard for the facts, and a lack of substance concerning meaningful issues. He repeated his hyperbolic shouts and baseless claims to groups apparently easily influenced as well as to high-value Republican donors. He threw chum in the water to incite his base while convincing its members that he walked on water, and they "drank his Kool-Aid" Jim Jones–style.[30]

What were they hearing? What did they truly understand about Trump? Were these people simply parroting Trump's statements, or did they take the time to investigate and arrive at informed opinions? Trump's victory surprised the most seasoned political pundits, members of Congress, and probably Trump himself. What else could explain it? He had no understanding of the office or the Constitution. He was no longer the controlling game-show host. He was soon to be lost in the swamp he vowed to drain.

Yes, he ran against Hillary Clinton, the country's first female candidate for president and presumed victor. Her use of a private email server at her home, questions about classified information circulating as a result, and the subsequent FBI investigations and announcements did not help her cause. Trump of course pounced on the email investigation and never let go, and to this day, he relives the election at every opportunity to deflect inquiries or to attack the Democratic Party. He finds himself on the other side of the table now as the investigation of his potential campaign links to Russia and other potential obstruction of justice charges are in the hands of a DOJ special prosecutor.

Not to be forgotten is the proven Russian meddling in the period leading up to the election. The intelligence community made this clear to Trump in a briefing after the election, but he apparently did not accept their conclusions and informed judgment. He reportedly showed little interest and did not ask how the meddling had occurred. He was the president, so by not knowing the details or denouncing the Russian interference, he provided a tacit endorsement of continued Russian interference in the 2018 midterms and potentially his 2020 campaign. That was an immediate warning from the intelligence community; Trump's not showing interest was perhaps a thank-you note to Putin. Proof positive in terms of election outcome voting has not yet come up, but clearly, there was a massive effort in play directed from Russia in support of Trump, and Putin has since admitted that he wanted Trump to win.

By her own admission, Clinton made mistakes during the campaign particularly in terms of her lack of connectivity with elements of the voting public and limited or no campaigning activity in important key states. Yet in spite of these shortcomings, her popular vote total was nearly three million more than Trump's. She had been in the public view for decades and most recently as secretary of state during Obama's first term in office. That experience along with her tenure as a senator from New York and as first lady and her interest in, knowledge of, and service to her country qualified her to be a candidate for the office. What wasn't anticipated in her campaign nor paid adequate attention to was that she was viewed as dishonest, corrupt, vindictive, and arrogant. Isn't it interesting that these same descriptors are now frequently applied to Trump and his presidency?

During the campaign, Trump brazenly and routinely confirmed that his knowledge of government was minimal, but that apparently did not deter his base of supporters. Through the years prior to his presidential bid, he was known for finding ways to circumvent loopholes in laws to financially benefit his business or in other ways obstruct opposition to his real estate desires through lawsuits and legal wrangling of the highest order. The credit for the majority of his wins and personal successes should probably most appropriately go to his accountants and attorneys as he pushed them to the edge of the sustained employee cliff and perhaps ethical abuse.

In spite of the decidedly negative history that surrounded

Trump personally and professionally, he convinced himself that he would be the best-ever president for the country, and a large percentage of voters in key states supported him.

> Many Trump supporters very legitimately feel that it is they who have been facing an unfair reality. The left needs to stop ignoring people's inner pain and fear. The racism, sexism and xenophobia used by Mr. Trump to advance his candidacy does not reveal an inherent malice in the majority of Americans.[31]

Perhaps not, but the recognition and implicit approval that Trump's tactics were acceptable deeply disturbs those who believe in historic and essential American principles.

As is becoming apparent, those who lined up behind Trump to "guide" him as he formally entered the primaries shared his enthusiasm for manipulation, name-calling, and believing a supposed successful businessperson could build a great society. Of course, that would play well with Trump as any stroke of his enormous ego must be true.

They all missed the point. The nation has demonstrated for over two centuries that opportunity for individual success exists in this country because the society is strong. Trump should understand that as president, he should encourage and support American society, not divide it and destroy its roots as he invokes deranged tantrums as policy. Internationally, his reputation is weak, and as former secretary of state Madeline Albright has stated in reference to Trump, "The chair of the leader of the free world is empty."[32]

Controversies continued for Trump before he took office. In many instances, the people he selected for his cabinet were billionaire cronies. Although Trump frequently stated that he knew more than the generals did, military members began to appear as potential cabinet members. Although over time he has surrounded himself with generals in nonmilitary positions, it appears that he rarely listens to them about policy, strategy, or action initiatives. The original national security adviser, Michael Flynn, resigned after twenty-three days on the job under a cloud of controversy regarding his interactions with Russia during and after the campaign and his lying to the vice president. Observing Trump during this period was a soap opera that broadcast the administration's blatant dismissal of facts genuinely hard to hide or being ignored by others.

Trump's "Day One promises"[33] made during his campaign were often repeated with bravado, threats, and demeaning verbal attacks on anyone or anything he believed were counter to his opinions or plan of action. His delivery on these promises was decidedly poor. Instead, he immediately signed a series of executive orders many of which produced little immediate impact of consequence, others that could not be implemented in a short time frame, and others that required the application of law. But yes, Trump does love photo opportunities. Americans are forced to watch the never-ending pen strokes of signing his name, a signature more appropriate for a billboard than a document, his show-and-tell holding of the documents for photographers, and then stumbling for something to say about what the order addressed. At times, based on his comments, it appeared he had not actually read them. His executive orders have been predominantly symbolic, and on more than one occasion, he started to leave the gatherings without remembering to sign the documents.

Has Trump been successful in following through with all his promises? Decidedly not, but for a new administration, this was not that surprising. It takes time to become established with people and procedures. Has Trump provided any details that put any meat on the bones of any of his promises? Not really. His own party leaders have voiced that concern about topics such as health care and tax reform.

The most obvious example is his promise for the repeal and replacement of the existing health care legislation, but that has not occurred. Though congressional leaders proposed many alternatives, Trump apparently did not offer any substantive contributions to what became a highly controversial legislative process. He could only muster up the words *repeal and replace* endlessly. He was quick to blame others for the failure. Republicans in Congress drafted more than one piece of legislation, worked in secret from the rest of Congress, and saw their tactics to push through legislation blocked. Ultimately, some started to retreat from blindly supporting the president. It is probably safe to say that the tension between Trump and Congress, both sides of the aisle, is real and a daily roller-coaster ride.

Trump has a substantial void when it comes to understanding and working collaboratively to develop meaningful legislation that Congress would approve particularly about those he droned on about during the campaign such as the Affordable Care Act (ACA). His obsession with the repeal and replacement of Obamacare looks to be more of a personal vendetta even as legislation has failed in Congress. It appears that Trump does not understand how the ACA works, and he does not have the personal ability to contribute to something new. Nonetheless, he has floated inflated, mistaken, and false statistics in his attempt to appear knowledgeable. He has dug such a deep hole on the topic and created even more partisan divides in Congress that his influence on health care legislation has been minimal, and yet he blames others, which demonstrates more of his deflections and distractions. Failure on his repeal and replace boast has since gathered a layer of dust as he moved on to other topics.

The absurdity Trump perpetuates regarding stalls and failings in Congress is directed predominantly toward Democrats as the reason things are not moving forward on any front, and not surprisingly, the blame for that is horribly misplaced. Trump's use of absolutes in his statements and attacks is almost comical. He of course does not view anything he's said or done as contributing factors to the lack of progress. Though his party is in a majority position, it has found it difficult to offset any Democratic resistance in Congress because Trump cannot restrain himself from demonstrating all manner of inappropriate behavior and rhetoric. As one member of Congress noted, "He needs adult supervision before he tweets or says anything."[34]

During the campaign, Trump made specific promises in his one-hundred-day plan, and although he has fulfilled some, the majority have not been realized, and he has not addressed others. His travel ban embarrassed the country as did his ill-informed, disrespectful conversations with the leaders of other countries. His most notable accomplishments have been the confirmation of Justices Neil Gorsuch and Brett Kavanaugh to the Supreme Court. Gorsuch received assistance by the "nuclear option" Republicans in Congress effected that eliminated the sixty-vote requirement for approval. Kavanaugh's confirmation hearings provided a spotlight on and the absurdity of partisan politics. Since his election, Trump has walked away from the first-hundred-days metric measurement that has been historically applied to presidencies and even now does not take ownership of a defined plan at all.

Most of Trump's first hundred days was an exhibition of naiveté, not that his lack of knowledge has decreased in any large measure. Administration appointments precipitated concerns particularly the appointment of Steve Bannon to the National

Security Council. Staff and advisers showed their inexperience, the national security adviser resigned amid controversy, and some cabinet nominees withdrew their names from consideration. The concept of a transition team was largely ignored because listening to inexperienced folks gave Trump more control through his wisdom. Wrong.

Trump himself contributed to the rocky start of his presidency through his remarks about the Muslim community, his clumsy approaches to a biased travel ban, criticizing a federal judge because of his heritage, accusing his predecessor of wiretapping phones in Trump Tower, offending foreign leaders, the attorney general recusing himself from the Russia collusion investigation, and more. What do these actions say about his decision-making proficiency and ability?

What the public may not have noticed are his appointments to federal courts and what that can mean for the future of the country. He has alienated those who could be helpful to him and routinely accepts no personal responsibility for anything that does not go his way. On the other hand, he rapidly takes credit for positive developments that he had nothing at all to do with in terms of specific contributions.

> *The most dangerous of all moral dilemmas: when we are obliged to conceal truth in order to help the truth to be victorious.*[35]

—Dag Hammarskjold

The only truth that matters to Trump is his own. Trump, and for now the Republican majority in Congress, can actually create positive outcomes if they put aside their collective partisan approach and personal agendas and allow ethical behavior to lead the way. The public should not view every Democratic question as unimportant or obstructionist when in reality their concerns are real and represent far more than the opposition party's view.

It's far too late for Trump to save face. He must put his ego and the power of the office on the back burner and move accountability and responsibility to the front. The chaos that begins with Trump and runs rampant in the White House is more than enough substantiation for both parties, the media, and Americans to have the right to ask questions, and the president has the responsibility to answer truthfully.

After less than a month in office, Trump began holding rallies that in effect were the beginnings of an election campaign for 2020 and meant to display himself as a hero to his supporters. He had shown no evidence of any accomplishment, and once again, he led with portraying how great he was, saying the things that created his patented distractions (building a wall, etc.), and continuing to incite his base, but he did nothing to demonstrate he understood how to fulfill the responsibilities of his office. His rationale for the rallies must not have included any strategy beyond fanning the flames of his divisive behavior. To make the leap to working on his political future when he could not point to anything that was constructive so early in his presidency was quite remarkable, and there began a string of less-than-positive events.

Less than a month after his inauguration, he held a rally in Florida; prior to that, National Security Adviser Michael Flynn resigned amid controversy. Roughly a month later, he traveled to Tennessee, and just prior to that, Attorney General Jeff Sessions recused himself from the Russia collusion investigation. Five days later in Kentucky, Trump accused President Obama of wiretapping him.

His next rally took place in Pennsylvania, and around that time, focus on his son-in-law and senior adviser Jared Kushner began regarding the Russia investigation and prior global financial dealings. In Iowa about forty days later, Trump announced his intent for the United States to withdraw from the Paris Climate Accord.

Then it was on to Ohio roughly a month later, and during that period, controversies surfaced around Trump's attendance at the G20 Summit (e.g., Ivanka sitting in for him at an important meeting, as well as his private, unaccompanied meetings with President Putin). A few days later, the special counsel leading the election collusion investigation issued grand jury subpoenas. And one day later, Trump began a seventeen-day vacation at one of his golf clubs.

For the first four or so months, Trump was holding a rally each month and continuing to relive the election campaign as he clearly had nothing substantive to say that in any way demonstrated progress or knowledge of any type on any level, but look deeper and consider what else was occurring in his sphere. The chaos of the Trump White House began to reach increasing levels of incompetence, and gaps in the timing of the rallies widened. His son-in-law came under increased scrutiny, and his son Donald Jr. became a focus because of a somewhat clandestine meeting at Trump Tower both having to do with Russian ties before, during, and after the campaign. He had announced the United States' intention to withdraw from the climate change accord to the astonishment of leaders around the globe, and his private, unsupervised meetings with Putin at the time remained somewhat suspect. Concurrently, he realized that he couldn't continue to stonewall his campaign and members of his inner circle, so he reinvigorated an attack in the form of distractions and deflections. As these investigations continue, it appears that details Trump may want to hide, including content from his publicly undisclosed tax returns, are becoming connected in ways that Congress and the public has not yet seen.

His initial post-inauguration rallies were attended by supporters and the curious in a range of 6,500–18,000, the larger number occurring in Louisville. Trump's base, most of the rally attendees of course, continue to reflect an over 40 percent approval rating. Over time, this range seems not to change dramatically regardless of how disjointed Trump and his actions occur on any particular topic. Trump's Teflon coating is quite remarkable; it doesn't seem to matter whether his supporters are unemployed or wealthy conservatives who can afford to accept Trump's reckless actions in the White House. His total disregard of political correctness on any level, his offending world leaders, and his inability to let go of Hillary Clinton as a constant distraction are all overlooked or worse just accepted by his supporters as a way to "make America great again."

It is objectively difficult to imagine that Trump will ever rid himself of the massive and detrimental voids he has created across a range of audiences. Will he gain the confidence of Congress, the public, and the world? This is an extremely difficult question to answer as the likelihood of additional missteps is significant just based on his personality. Trump would clearly need to put the country before himself.

The inexperience if not the lack of skill of many of his inner-circle advisers and staff members, statements from loyal family members and their miscues, and his tweets, posts, and interviews demonstrate Trump's management style; it defaults to bullying, accusing, and criticizing. Americans are witnessing Trump's obvious lack of suitably for the office; he can and does embarrass the United States and is potentially leading it and its citizens into a multi-level abyss. The dysfunction in the Trump White House is continual. Infighting between staffers, personality clashes with

Trump appointees and family members, and a lack of meaningful communication with Congress undermine any confidence in the Trump administration.

The federal government requires competent people at many levels to be confirmed, accept appointments, and so forth as efficiently as possible. After one year in office, Trump is behind his predecessor in the number of nominations and confirmations for positions in the courts and agencies.[36] The changing cast of characters in the White House, Trump's notable lack of skill in working with others, and his lack of understanding the government and its working parts make the timing for establishing a fully staffed government difficult to predict. Trump is a lost soul; he has not studied his lines and responsibilities as the true leader of the country. In his first year in office, Trump had a 34 percent turnover in his first-tier staff.[37]

Trump appears unprepared when reading from a page of notes or prepared text, and he strives to demonstrate his knowledge as he continually ad-libs the same tired and simplistic lines that communicate little and show his endless need to sound important. In the process, however, that exposes him as being far from presidential and even confuses the purpose of his message. He grabs his shoulders for a hug and dives into content he has not studied and does not fully understand.

Trump's speechwriters, having made him his advisers' mouthpiece in some regards, attempt to make him appear more competent with the material but in fact have accomplished just the opposite. His comments laced with criticism directed toward them has shocked world leaders and accomplished little. Should a coalition of nations be required in the future to face a worldwide threat, Trump does not have the capability of gathering world support particularly when he ignores his military and intelligence communities.

Two or three long-standing allies may not be enough as their interests are as critical to their position in the world order as is that of the US. He has called other leaders, exaggerated the significance of these calls, and in the process done little to establish solid relationships with them. Trump has shown that he is not a student of history—presidential, congressional, country, or world—and is apparently not well read, making it arduous for others to trust his opinions.

Trump is suspected of having ongoing conflicts of interests between his prior life and his presidency. Some would seem to be blatantly obvious and have raised the topic of the Constitution's emoluments clause. Others are as yet cloaked by Trump and his attorneys' maneuverings, but all nevertheless are troublesome for intelligent and reliable experts, including constitutional scholars. "Follow the money" is a far too logical approach in Trump's case. For example, his tax returns, to this point hidden away, will provide insights and answers. There are far too many questions to be asked and answered for Trump to ultimately disguise or hide. The special counsel investigation may provide perspective and answers on many fronts.

Trump's original press secretary was so intent in purveying Trumpspeak that he quickly established a lack of credibility as well. As a conduit for Trump, he served most successfully in widening the gap between the president, the media, the American public, and the global community. Trump moved Sean Spicer aside; he later resigned, and Trump thrust the deputy press secretary upon the world. Sarah Huckabee Sanders has stepped in with observable confidence as press secretary but with little favorable response from the media or the public; her condescending demeanor does little to establish her as a trusted and credible source of information, nor has her parroting of Trump false claims.

Next came another example of Trump's focus on friendship

and loyalty rather than on expertise and appropriateness for a position. Trump appointed Anthony Scaramucci as White House communications director; he was a business friend and successful financial hedge-fund manager. Scaramucci, the Mooch, immediately raised more questions than he provided answers, and he did not inspire any confidence in the White House's ability or willingness to communicate openly to the American public. Although a successful and intelligent financial manager, his fast talk, big gestures and a style more appropriate for a used-car salesman provided no confidence that this appointment was going to work, and it didn't.

Shortly thereafter, the original chief of staff left the White House under somewhat not fully exposed circumstances, but inner-circle disagreements are suspected to be the reason. His replacement came from the cabinet, Secretary John Kelly, who was historically respected for his leadership in the Marine Corps and more recently as Trump's selection as the leader of the Department of Homeland Security. In very short order, he recommended that the Mooch be fired after ten days of chaos. Some have speculated that a primary factor for the dismissal was Scaramucci's language that offended Trump's wife and daughter. If that is true, it is interesting that this level of family members' disdain did not apply to Trump's *Access Hollywood* statements about women.

Another disturbing component of the entry of Kelly and the exit of Scaramucci was the coverage given to the immediate impact of Kelly's appointment rather than the incredulous lack of insight demonstrated by Trump in hiring Scaramucci in the first place. It seems that Trump was out of touch with the abilities an effective White House communications director had to have. Trump's well-established need for loyalty from his underlings may have led to his hiring decision and an assumption that all of his appointees would be loyal.

It is challenging to determine what Trump has truly encouraged through study, sound thinking, and development of detailed proposals that take into account their true potential impact on our country and world. One must also question the input and motives of his inner circle. If Trump, as some in Congress have implied, is a child running through the hallways of the White House, someone who cares about this country needs to trip him quickly and give him a proverbial time-out. Threats. Posturing. Contemptable distractions. Apparently, some elements of his base of supporters believe this is the way positive change occurs and is responsible behavior for a president.

Glimpses of Trump's behavior serve as slap-in-the-face realizations of the size of Trump's self-image. Opposition to his opinions is apparently unacceptable. His day-to-day approach to the office demonstrates his lack of understanding of how to accomplish an agenda with Congress even with a majority of his party in the driver's seat. He has shown no interest in true communication with the entire population as he evidently listens only to himself and tweets for himself and his base. Trump has reached the point of even alienating members of his own party with the exception of a few who are so careful with their words that they are looking to be viewed favorably by Trump for some potential future endorsement or appointment. In comparison, some Republicans in Congress have gone on record that they doubt Trump's capacity and competence as president.

Other Republicans are hiding in plain view hoping not to so alienate voters that they won't be reelected, and they fear coming under Trump's direct attack. For example, Trump's reversal of support and outward criticism of his attorney general, who by the way he nominated and was his first supporter from the Senate. It was not a surprise when Trump ultimately fired the leader of the DOJ after the 2018 midterm elections. Trump has been forced to realize and accept that the attorney general is not there to protect him. Many feel Sessions did the right thing by recusing himself regarding the Russian investigation though he should be held accountable for not remembering his own interactions with the Russian ambassador during the campaign period.

Trump tends to criticize anyone connected with the Russia investigation, including several DOJ employees, the director of the FBI, the deputy attorney general, and the special prosecutor. He is apparently enraged about the investigation into his and his family's financial history and potential suspicious relationships with others in this country and abroad as reported in a *New York Times* interview.[38]

Trump's patent response to criticism as he sinks further into dysfunction involves threatening to fire someone while spreading further distractions. What he has found, however, is that some of those in his crosshairs have ethics his threats won't erode. Robert S. Muller III the special prosecutor in the possible Russian interference investigation, has likely found more and more avenues to pursue, some surfacing from the frank callousness of Trump and his family. The varied controversies surrounding Donald Jr. and Jared Kushner have become intertwined with Trump, and statements by the White House and Trump himself have resulted in increased suspicions. It is quite impossible to predict where the special prosecutor's investigation will lead and what substantiated conclusions will be drawn, but the apparent breadth and extended length of the investigation is significant.

Trump and some in his inner circle must be staying awake at night thinking about grand juries, subpoenas, and federal charges being filed against them. The guilty outcomes on charges against his former campaign manager, Paul Manafort, and his former personal attorney, Michael Cohen, in federal court proceedings may be only the beginning.

At the same time the special counsel was conducting its examinations, the Senate and House Intelligence Committee investigations were underway; they focused on Russian interventions in the election, though these two panels have operated quite differently when measured by ethical standards. Trump tweeted some controversial statements about the investigations, and each committee has nevertheless been obligated to comment.

The most recent noise created by highly partisan letters being released on some topics has heightened the intrigue. The Republican-dominated House Committee called its investigation to an end with conclusions that seemed to ignore the most obvious facts. It makes one think that the Trump potholes are deeper in his administration's streets than can be imagined, but partisan protection will go only so far.

Trump believes only in what his fleeting thoughts are at any moment, and these thoughts result in a brutalization of the government, the economy, institutions, global allies, and individuals. It is quite impossible for him to stay on any point for long. He is a verbal accident waiting to happen, and he demonstrated this during the primary debates. He believes diplomacy is having the strongest handshake followed by a complete lack of insightful and "unpresidented (sic)"[39] preparation for any discussion with a world leader, and stunningly, Trump does not reflect the ethical base, history, and reputation of the United States. His statements during the campaign about his views on other countries were embarrassing as they came from a remarkably uninformed individual. He has continued to demonstrate his uneducated view since he has been in office, and that does nothing to foster positive opinions of him around the world.

Trump continues to arouse fear in many forms but with one common denominator—he speaks without or misuses facts and tries hard to create an image of knowing what he is doing. The problem: a minute-to-minute analysis of what he says would provide little to support this view. As more questions are raised about his past, including the workings of his campaign and personal relationships, one additional constant is that his ethics are subject to question as are the defenses, most frequently denials, that are put forward for his actions by himself or his attorneys. When his mental ability came under question, he responded,

> Actually, throughout my life, my two greatest assets have been mental stability and being, like, really smart. Crooked Hillary Clinton also played these cards very hard and, as everyone knows, went down in flames. I went from VERY successful businessman, to top T.V. Star, to President of the United States (on my first try). I think that would qualify as not smart, but genius....and a very stable genius at that![40]

Trump has played these cards, the fire is lit, and he too is on a path of an increasingly self-destruction as his actions don't support his assessment of himself.

Just prior to Trump's inauguration, the US Office of Government Ethics published an amended regulation titled Standards of Ethical Conduct for Employees of the Executive Branch.[41] A section of this regulation, Basic Obligation of Public Service,[42] in its general principles section begins with this: "Public service is a public trust requiring employees to place loyalty to the Constitution, the laws and ethical principles above private gain." Trump's lack of an organized, experienced, and capable transition team may have overlooked the standards of ethical conduct entirely.

Absence of public trust in Trump is a concern frequently

voiced by numerous demographic components of American society because his avoidance of facts does not foster belief in what he says at any point. This obligation section of the regulation goes on to cover areas such as "shall not hold financial interests that conflict with conscientious performance of duty." Although information may ultimately be forthcoming from the Department of Justice investigation, examination of tax returns, and so forth, it is safe to profess that separation from his financial interests is the essence of this conduct statement.

"Employees shall put forth honest effort in the performance of their duties." The public sees considerable arm-waving and empty boasts from Trump that are hard to assess as representative of an honest effort of a president adhering to the ethics conduct policy.

The last general principle listed in the regulation is of particular concern considering all that has transpired thus far in the Trump presidency.

> Employees shall endeavor to avoid any actions creating the appearance that they are violating the law or the ethical standards set forth in this part. Whether particular circumstances create an appearance that the law of these standards have been violated shall be determined from the perspective of a reasonable person with knowledge of the relevant facts.

These statements do make one wonder how Trump would sidestep a challenge by a reasonable person with knowledge of the relevant facts. A topic of ongoing discussion is the numerous "appearances" that he is violating the law or ethical standards. The special counsel leading the investigation into several areas of Russian interference in the 2016 election is more than qualified to do so; Mueller investigation will parse the relevant facts. Election conspiracy and obstruction of justice are the primary column headings for the investigation as it relates to law. Ethical standards are another matter entirely and in comparison may be a relatively easier path to pursue.

The troublesome Trump presidency raises new issues almost daily and sometimes more frequently. They fall into two predominant categories: ludicrous statements and missteps by the president himself, or a statement or action his staff or cabinet members have precipitated. Most if not all provide no upside for the country; just the opposite. A common ground for both categories is the combination of Trump presenting his "I am the expert" approach with others agreeing with him or attempting to guide him in the right direction. At the same time, some of these individuals are facing their own alleged indiscretions in the boundaries of their responsibilities and budgets. In their own ways, they are manipulating the country to their advantage.

Immediately after Trump's election and certainly after he took the oath of office, the stings of the office began to accumulate. The embarrassment of the Michael Flynn fiasco was just the first. Trump had a paranoid fixation on FBI director James Comey's testimony before the Senate Intelligence Committee about the counterintelligence investigation into Russian meddling in the election. He allegedly asked Director of National Intelligence Dan Coats and CIA Director Mike Pompeo to intervene with Comey, which they declined to do. Trump subsequently (March 30, 2017) asked Comey to "lift the cloud" of the Russia investigation and asked him to announce publicly that he was not under investigation. In a call days later (April 1, 2017), Trump allegedly asked Comey to again make it clear he was not under investigation. Do Trump's repetitive actions in this matter suggest he was unconcerned about what investigations might surface, or was it paranoia at play?

Trump had consistently denied Russian collusion and chose only to deflect attention to Clinton's emails and anything else he could come up with to distract the public following his election.

On May 17, 2017, Acting Attorney General Rod Rosenstein appointed Mueller as the special counsel for the Department of Justice.[43] Rosenstein's appointment of Mueller listed three main areas of investigation that were confirmed by then FBI Director Comey's testimony before the House Select Committee on Intelligence on March 20, 2017. These were any links and/or coordination between the Russian government and individuals associated with Trump's campaign, any matters that arose or might arise directly from the investigation, and any other matters within the scope of 28 C.F.R. § 600.4(a).[44]

Lest it be overlooked, Trump had fired Comey eight days previously on May 9, 2017 but denied that the Russia investigation was a factor. However, before a national television audience on May 12, 2017, in an interview with NBC's Lester Holt, his description of the Comey firing was quite different.

> When I decided to just do it I said to myself, I said, you know, this Russia thing, with Trump and Russia, is a made-up story, it's an excuse for the Democrats to have lost an election that they should have won.[45]

This one sentence is quite remarkable in that Trump clearly established a relationship between the firing of Comey and the Russia investigation. Further, he also appeared to admit that he understood going into the election that he should not have been elected. Even in the face of his own words admitting that the investigation was a factor in the firing of Comey, over a year later, he continues to state the opposite.

So what has this uncommon, ethically questionable, accidental president wrought? For now, there is no clear or consensus answer. He unfortunately is a work in progress; predicting any Trump outcome with finality is exceedingly difficult. Some will follow this Piped Piper off the cliff while others sit back and believe everything will be all right. Still others are genuinely and rightfully concerned about where the country is headed under Trump's irregular ramblings, uninformed pronouncements, and actions. The US is facing pressing matters at home and important and risky challenges abroad, but the president spends the better part of his waking moments acting out in multiple ways that offer little actionable substance. He constantly criticizes others, including his own appointees to the judiciary, those in the legislative branch, his cabinet members, and the operations of essential government agencies, including the FBI.

Through his propensity to tweet, Trump has assaulted the fabric of this country, including its morality and religions. His tweets lack facts, and through them, he twists, insults, exaggerates, incites, and lies. Some argue that Trump's victory was not an accident; they believe his strategic approach to the election was epic. Inciting violence at rallies is hardly strategic; it's more a matter of appealing to a cohort of Americans who may not study in depth to understand issues but get easily caught up in Trump's sporting-event mentality. The election should have been about the country's future, not threats to the Second Amendment or making misogynistic remarks about his opponent. A weak and highly flawed individual made the appeal for victory that has become an embarrassment for the country and its standing in the world.

All men make mistakes, but a good man yields when he knows his course is wrong and repairs the evil. The only crime is pride.[46]

Determining right and wrong may be difficult for Trump. He may not care about the difference; continuing down a corridor of mistakes may be his standard operating procedure. He may just prefer whatever course of the moment works for him evil or not. He may not consider the consequences of his actions or doesn't care, and historically in his personal sphere, he has depended on others to fix mistakes, cover up his missteps, and personally join him in twisting the truth. He is led by his ego wherever that may lead the country. Trump does not shy away from conflict and often encourages it. "This is how he won," according to former chief strategist Stephen Bannon. "This is how he governs, and this is his 'superpower.' Drama, action, emotional power."[47]

The cross-section of Americans paying attention to Trump, Congress, and government agencies may well have reached a higher level of interest than in the past. Fear is a great motivator. There are so many topics of elevated concern that various demographic groups are staying more informed about Trump's actions and inactions viewed as threatening to their morals, livelihood, and lifestyle. A reliance on journalists is more important than ever as these professionals serve willingly in their watchdog role concerning the government. In the meantime, those who choose only to be Trump's cheerleaders will have little basis for complaining when they realize their cheers have promoted more chaos, little positive change and contributions to America and "greatness."

"I am not at all concerned that anyone in the world can look at the United States and understand it to be anything but a beacon of hope, democracy and freedom," secretary of state Mike Pompeo said in an exclusive telephone interview marking his first two months in office. "We have a long history of that and it has continued under the Trump administration."[48] Really?

Pompeo must be watching a different movie. The things he suggests are continuing under Trump are missing from his playbook. The consensus of positive world opinion he alludes to would be hard to quantify. Trump's win philosophy has trampled the hopes of many, threatened the principles of democracy, and only display his narrow view of what freedom means.

A dramatic accident has happened in America—a train wreck of massive proportions with cars still leaving the tracks. The damage to Americans and the long-term outcome for the country is terribly uncertain.

CHAPTER 2

OZ WAS MAKE-BELIEVE

Do not meddle in the affairs of wizards, for they are subtle and quick to anger.[49]

Donald J. Trump is the forty-fifth president of the United States, but many find that fact difficult to acknowledge and increasingly harder to accept. How Trump arrived at that historically respected and revered executive office has become even more difficult to comprehend since his inauguration. His unorthodox behavior in seeking support during the primaries and election campaign resonated with some factions of the voting public. He constructed his personal crusade around breaking all the rules of campaigning, debate, and decorum.

Since his election, his unconventional and sometimes bizarre behavior as president has continued to the detriment of the country. His shortage of governing experience and competence and his repeated failure to use a congressional advantage to accomplish meaningful progress for the country are notable. Troublesome revelations surface with alarming frequency. Logically connecting the dots of his shouted scheme of governing is quite impossible. The country constantly faces more Trump dots presented most commonly as inaction or distractions that confuse or camouflage clear and informed direction. Perhaps it is helpful to evaluate Trump and those around him in terms of a classic entertainment example, the genre he also perceives as an unchallenged area of his expertise.

In the classic 1939 film adaptation of *The Wonderful World of Oz*,[50] Dorothy faces a variety of challenges, including Ms. Gulch, who took Dorothy's dog, Toto, for chasing her cat. Dorothy feels her Aunt Em and Uncle Henry are not supporting her, so she runs away. She encounters Professor Marvel, who quickly surmises her situation and encourages her to return home. On her way home, a tornado touches down, and she is rendered unconscious. Her detachment with reality begins. It is unclear, however, where Trump's detachment with truth, authenticity, and reality began.

In her dream, Dorothy awakes in Munchkin Land and learns her home has fallen on the Wicked Witch of the East and killed her. The Munchkins treat Dorothy as a hero for ridding their land of the Wicked Witch. She meets the mayor, the Lollipop Gang, the Munchkin coroner, and various Munchkin villagers who are very happy her fall from the star of Kansas resulted in their independence from the Wicked Witch of the East. Glenda, the Good Witch, magically removes the Wicked Witch of the East's special ruby slippers and places them on Dorothy's feet. She emboldens Dorothy to find her way home by beginning her journey down the Yellow Brick Road to the Emerald City, where she will meet the Wizard of Oz.

Without retelling the story in its entirety, consider the similar circumstance in which the Trump administration exists. The Library of Congress has designated the movie adaptation "America's greatest and best-loved fairytale." It is difficult to fathom that any such favorable description from any source other than Trump would declare such high praise for the Trump presidency, but "most-damaging nightmare" may be the explanation applied by many others. Today, the American public in effect is the new Dorothy caught up in the chaotic world of Trumpism with no magic slippers in sight. Americans would very much like to go home to a respectful society based on core values, but like Dorothy, they may well end up as twenty-first-century orphans; but hopefully only as a temporary condition.

By Trump's account, the country was a disaster as he took office. He had difficulty leaving his home(s), be it Trump Tower in New York City, other hotels, golf clubs, and so on, to take up residence at the White House. Rumor had it that he referred to the White House as a dump—not enough gold perhaps. Of course, he later walked back that comment and attempted civility by describing how beautiful the White House was and how comfortable he was living there. This is a simplistic example of how Trump swings in his thinking, but unfortunately, it is consistently evident in his assessments of more-serious subjects.

The Trump fairytale remains an evolving and sorry picture of the presidency that illustrates just how out of place he is. He has little knowledge of protocol and a quite marked proclivity to insult individuals and countries. He acts more like a critic and villain of America than a rational and reasonable president. He routinely vocalizes ragged, extemporaneous thoughts that are difficult to follow and that lack facts. When confronted with opposition to his statements based on facts, he retreats to his bully posture as it is quite impossible for him to accept he could be wrong. Early on, Republican Paul Ryan, the Speaker of the House, made what has become a memorable excuse for Trump: "He's just new at this."[51] Trump obviously has learned little since then.

A case could be made that Trump equates the media as his

personal Wicked Witch of the West (the one on the broomstick); shortly after his inauguration, he stated that the press was the enemy of the people.[52] He repeats this statement frequently and continues his attack against the First Amendment with great regularity. More recently, Trump stated on Twitter, "Our country's biggest enemy is the fake news so easily promulgated by fools."[53] Trump is outraged and befuddled by information leaks, many apparently from inside the White House and others originating from governmental agencies. He overlooks the fact that he is the leaker-in-chief owing to his mismanagement of personnel, his total inability to stay on point evidenced by non sequiturs at news conferences, and the conflicting direction he gives to his communications staff. And then of course there are his tweets— bizarre and repeatedly false declarations. When his errors (false claims, lies, etc.) are pointed out, he becomes enraged. He must think that his words are golden and above being questioned regardless of their obvious lack of reality or reliability. The media and the Democrats become the subjects of his attacks regardless of the facts.

Parallels are easily drawn to Oz and the original Trump senior staffers who came aboard lacking diplomatic and governmental experience. They are representative of the famous characters needing help—the Scarecrow who lacks a brain, the Tin Woodsman who lacks a heart, and the Cowardly Lion who lacks courage.

It's difficult to avoid noticing Vice President Mike Pence's constantly squinting eyes and furrowed brow. President Lyndon Johnson advised,

> *Watch their hands, watch their eyes. Read eyes. No matter what a man is saying to you, it's not as important as what you can read in his eyes. The most important thing a man has to tell you is what he's not*

*telling you; the most important thing he has to say is
what he's trying not to say.*[54]

—President Lyndon Johnson

That's good counsel when it comes to observing Pence
and many others in the continuously updated list of Trump
administration officials. Pence's outwardly painful appearance
as he visibly lurks in the background of most photographs of
Trump and peering around corners and doorways in the White
House is not necessarily vice presidential but emphatically hard to
miss. Several interpretations can be made. Pence may be thinking
through the scenarios of his next career move following Trump's
abandonment by the Republican Party, Trump's impeachment
or resignation, or his next move if criminal charges are brought
against Trump. In the meantime, his over-the-top compliments
about Trump come off as mundane and pointless.

Lest they be forgotten, consider the Munchkin family members
who became part of Trump's White House inner circle. Daughter
Ivanka was appointed assistant to the president. Son-in-law Jared
Kushner was appointed senior adviser to the president with a
governmental security clearance and was assigned "small" tasks
such as fixing everything that was wrong with the government and
solving international matters of importance such as negotiating
peace between Palestine and Israel. In spite of his resume of
inexperience for such challenges, he was his father-in-law's choice.

This daughter and son-in-law team continues in positions
of some influence however inappropriate. Frequently, like the
president, they embarrass the country, but in time, they have
become much less visible. These nepotistic appointments were of
concern to many as the US Code on such appointments makes its

concern about the current situation abundantly clear particularly in regard to conflicting business interests.[55]

There are many other Oz characters and Trump administration comparisons to be made, but it's most important to consider the Wizard. Trump quite obviously believes he is the wizard of all things—"I know more than the generals" and "I'm the only one who can fix it." Trump of course has no credibility as a wizard, and he should consider one very important fact—the Wizard in the book and movie was a fake. It's a fraternity.

Professor Marvel (a.k.a. the Wizard of Oz) was a common man who found himself exiled when his hot-air balloon faltered and he landed in Munchkin Land. He took up his disguise, fooled the residents, and became viewed as all powerful and wise. This description easily brings to mind the failures of some of Trump's business ventures, his nonsensical tweets, and his continuous outrageous hot-air comments he thrusts upon Americans and the world. A statement by Trump's first press secretary, Sean Spicer, read, "President Donald Trump's tweets are considered official statements by the President of the United States, because the president is the President of the United States."[56] This is so revealing in so many ways. Consider the sampling of early official statements below.

> Sorry losers and haters, but my I.Q. is one of the highest, and you know it! Please don't feel so stupid or insecure, it's not your fault.[57]

> (Whose fault is he implying it is?)

> How low has President Obama gone to tapp (*sic*) my phones during the very sacred election process. This is Nixon/Watergate. Bad (or sick) guy.[58]

(Interesting he should reference President Richard Nixon, isn't it?)

Crazy Joe Biden is trying to act like a tough guy. Actually, he is weak, both mentally and physically, and yet he threatens me, for the second time, with physical assault. He doesn't know me, but he would do down fast and hard, crying all the way.[59]

(Was he suggesting a duel at dawn?)

Trump boasts about the millions of his Twitter followers, yet it evades him that an overwhelming number of these digital devotees are undoubtedly waiting for his next despicable tweet as comic relief as opposed to receiving his wisdom or having any true admiration for the content or the man. The disturbing prospect of his ongoing 280-character rants is that they do provide insight into the mind of an individual whose personality does not build confidence in others.

There is no need for others in his administration to apply show-business exaggeration or create controversy to spawn confusion and outrage though there are many examples of his staff and appointees doing just that. The president has exaggeration and controversy well covered all by himself. With tweets being his primary communication tool such as it is, he has nothing to gain by prolonging his bully persona and expressions of his imperfect vocabulary. He seemingly cannot stop his pathological whining, and some have described him as living in an alternate universe. He was a political outsider elected to the country's highest office, and unfortunately for him, that may also include living alone in his own world, a bizarre fantasy world if you will.

Perhaps an *Alice's Adventures in Wonderland* [60] comparison is also applicable in an attempt to make some logical sense of what Trump is doing. Leading the country and its people down a rabbit hole is a feeling and a reality many share. Like Alice, Trump faces many locked doors, and as he has hopefully realized but perhaps ignored, he does not have a magic potion to make himself small to begin an unquestioned journey. Is Trump the Mad Hatter, the March Hare, or the Cheshire Cat? "Most everyone's mad here. You may have noticed that I'm not all there myself," says the Cheshire Cat.

Trump can't stop himself from issuing deflecting distractions when cornered to speak accurately and authoritatively though the American people are looking for truth and reassurance. Perhaps this is not a hundred percent accurate. If he were so inclined, he could stop this sort of common behavior, but he clearly chooses to remain controversial. He seems to enjoy inciting conflict and using smoke and mirrors when questions come up about his actions as president. Suspicions and concerns are on the table about his personal business interests beginning with his refusal to provide his tax returns as has been the common practice for presidents and candidates in recent history. And of course, he is not a fan of the special prosecutor appointed to investigate all manner of his personal involvements. He threatens and demeans historically important allies that the US needs on the world stage. He doesn't have the background or knowledge to appreciate the nuances of intelligence briefings. One page of bullet points as his means of truly understanding a situation is ludicrous if not sad as is looking to equally inexperienced and personal agenda–biased staffers for guidance. It is also apparent that his staff does not truly keep him objectively informed or take the position of just staying out of his way.

It would be welcomed if at least a part of the Wizard's movie dialogue, when he was exposed, could come to fruition in the

Trump world: "Pay no attention to that man behind the curtain," but is out for all to see and hear. In the future, however, bringing the curtain down on Trump may become an option.

Because of his election victory, the supposed wizard in the White House has the ideological and blind or at minimum the vision-impaired support of his party. He unmistakably demonstrates a lack of knowledge or interest in the application of the conservative principles that have guided and served that party for decades. This wizard's most visible supporters focus on their reelection, maintaining a majority voting bloc, and actively criticizing the Democratic Party just because. But as Trump has moved from one crisis to the next, the partisan mortar that holds even Republican support together has begun to crumble.

Frankly, the White House wizard is not a wizard at all. He lacks any positive attribute and complimentary wizard-like personal descriptors. In his version of an impossible movie script, Trump took the role of an accidental president at play. In this case, being assigned the title of wizard doesn't imply competency. In fear that what occurred during his campaign and since would be forgotten, this president has frequently shouted that elections were rigged. Well, he made it to the presidency, so he could be right as evidenced by the ongoing disclosures about Russian meddling and allegations of other inappropriate behavior. "We'll have to see." Enough said.

There is little evidence Trump has an even rudimentary knowledge of the Constitution, government management, or propriety. If he possessed any of these things and applied them appropriately, he might command the attention and respect of those looking for leadership and ethical behavior from a president. If he had interest in accessing this information, analyzing it, and arriving at an informed opinion, things might be productively different from what we have seen to date. Instead, in an Associated

Press interview, Trump stated, "I have a great relationship with Congress. I think we're doing very well and I think we have a great foundation for future things."[61] Thus far, this statement is difficult to accept much less prove.

Trump relies on his insiders—many of whom mirror his lack of experience and some of whom are frightening when reasonable people assess them. Trump does not command respect when he shoots from the hip with a well-developed deficit of personality or empathy. Likewise, many in his inner circle have not shown that they possess the sincere traits and moral character shown by Dorothy's insiders and friends such as Uncle Henry and Aunt Em, or Zeke Hunk and Hickory.

Can the electorate really be happy with Trump's staff choices? Will Trump's base ever face the fact that they support an alarmingly weak and unbalanced president? It's not about President Barak Obama's record, or Secretary Clinton as a lesser alternative candidate, or any other pathetic generalization in an attempt to justify his election. It's time to give those topics a rest and ask the hard questions about the future with Trump in office.

At a time when favorable opinion, confidence, honesty, competence, and ethics are sorely needed and expected, this self-proclaimed presidential wizard of the deal has consistently continued to deconstruct the image of the country as the world's superpower. This supposed wizard has elevated deception and distraction to a fine art at every turn and with the support of his cast of insiders. Trump's disapproval rating has ranged from 43 percent at his inauguration to 52 percent through mid-June 2018; it peaked thus far at 58 percent in August 2017.[62] With daily controversial occurrences, statements, and miscues, the Trump administration falls into its own chuckholes as the country and the world look on at Trump's personal Oz between the Pacific and the Atlantic.

Take a closer look at some of the Oz movie characters and how their circumstances identify with the Trump administration. A tornado had whisked Dorothy to Munchkin Land, and she wanted to find her way home. By comparison, state primaries delivered Trump, the candidate who was more inclined to entertainment and controversy and had a decided capacity to embarrass his party and be underestimated by his opponents. Dorothy and her friends were underestimated too as she later caused the witch to melt with a water bath. Trump's Achilles' heel is quite different; most likely, he will cause his own demise. "We'll have to see."

The Wicked Witch of the East, who was crushed by Dorothy's house, is known only for being the evil sister of the Wicked Witch of the West. Little was known about Trump other than the size of his property logos, his propensity to all things gold, exaggerations, multiple wives, and a library of allegations against him pointing to questioned business successes and failures.

Glenda, the Good Witch, represents good in the battle with evil. In Trump's Oz, we don't see much of any balance of these extremes or anyone on his staff with whom a suitable comparison can be made. The country and the world are exposed to his proclamations about how wonderful he is in so many ways and in any situation.

The Wicked Witch of the West focuses on Dorothy's red slippers much the way Trump fixates on the media. Just as she melted when good triumphed over evil, Trump is in a slow burn and melting by his own self-fulfilling prophecy.

The Scarecrow, the Tin Man, and the Cowardly Lion constituted a needy group of individuals—pick your own candidates from the administration—with their particular personality flaws and needs. Trump states he has a presidential agenda but has not been able to clearly communicate what it is other than through repetitious, headline-type statements. It's like watching the ebb and flow of the ocean; every wave is different from the one before. This metaphor is a fair interpretation of Trump. The White House staff, apparently threatened by Trump in some ways, features a cast of individuals playing against one another based on unpublished direction from Trump. The reporting of the infighting is showcased by White House leaks, embarrassing interactions with the media and media reports, and a constantly changing cast in the administration.

Professor Marvel creates the wizard facade that he is very knowledgeable, knows very important people, and does very important things. He employs his crystal ball to predict the future in a somewhat biased way as he proclaims that he has, "sneered at doom and chuckled at catastrophe."[63] Trump likes to describe himself in a similar way, and on multiple occasions, he referred to his many roles and his expertise "the likes of which the world has never been seen before." No argument there. The professor, eventually shown to be the Wizard in the movie, was a manipulator who was ultimately exposed. Trump is caught constantly through the onslaught of his ridiculous, egocentric tweets. The professor speaks to Toto "as one dog to another," and Trump has a kennel of players of his own making.

Due to his incessant belief that what he says will become true—"Believe me"—the presidency of the United States is under siege by someone who is singularly impressed by what he sees in the mirror and by those who stroke his need for adoration.

> *We're off to see the Wizard*
> *The Wonderful Wizard of Oz*
> *We hear he is a whiz of a Wiz*
> *If ever a Wiz there was ...*[64]

It is possible that some in the Trump administration believe these lyrics apply to the president. Perhaps they are just indicating a need for their medication dosages to be titrated upward. An exercise of cleansing realization for those who supported his election might be to write down anything substantively positive Trump has accomplished for their well-being—facts, not rhetoric. Talking tough, alienating allies, making racist remarks, and insulting anyone in this president's view should not appear on these lists, nor should the broad strokes of his pen that subsequently precipitated other problems but did not necessarily provide solutions.

> *Everyone is entitled to his own opinion, but not his own facts.*[65]

—Daniel Patrick Moynihan

Facts must be a rare priority for Trump. His insistence that media reports about his own statements are fake demonstrates a methodology of parsing words that only he understands—don't confuse me with the facts. Professional journalists fact-check statements about history, claims, data, and all manner of a story's components in an effort to be accurate, balanced, and fair. Editorials are reserved for the Op-Ed page. Trump's taking umbrage at those who report his statements and their deficiencies shows that for him, it's only a one-way legitimacy street and that the only street he travels is Trump Boulevard.

Over the years, he has diligently created his image or the Trump brand as some suggest. He has shown through his reported historic, questionable activities that the media could only observe, fact-check, and report how Trump constructed his ethical and moral profile. Prior to the presidency, the Trump brand demonstrated a history of performance and personal achievements that in some instances represented mistreatment of individuals and alleged dubious business practices by those he employed.

The residents of the Emerald City accepted the Wizard of Oz, but fortunately, Americans are not that gullible, or at least not an ongoing majority of them.

What about the Emerald City? It is ruled by the Wizard, who promotes himself through misrepresentations of his knowledge and power to fool the city's inhabitants. He communicates that he is all powerful, and he put fear in the minds of the people based on his boasts about his capacity to perform outstanding feats. In fact, he was powerless and ineffectual, and when Toto revealed him behind the curtain, he confessed, "I'm a very bad wizard."[66]

Is Trump a reincarnation of that Wizard? Just review the facts and examine his skill at producing "outstanding feats" and true accomplishments for the country beyond creating controversy. On the one hand, he was a natural for the role of wizard as his views of the world are as distorted as those of the movie Wizard were. Trump has not drained the swamp in Washington as he claimed he would do; rather, he has added a subdivision to it. As the fascist dictator Benito Mussolini ("Il Duce"– the Leader) was coming to power in Italy in the early 1900s, he shouted *drenare la palude*—drain the swamp. History accurately documents the circumstances of his ultimate fall from power.

Trump continues his unchallenged penchant for controversy through insults directed at members of Congress, institutions, foreign leaders and countries, ethnic groups, and even Americans who with each passing day are asking themselves, *What is he going to say next?* America need not worry about the president being sleepily awakened at three in the morning to hear about a nuclear threat; he will be up tweeting his daily barrage of insults but not expanding his content and vocabulary in the process. Any worry should focus on what he would do with the nuclear launch codes at his disposal.

It is almost impossible for the media to keep up with Trump's "deep thinking." Responsible coverage of his continuing missteps, misrepresentations, contradictions (and the administration's creation of flawed news), walk-backs, questionable past and current interactions, notable and suspected conflict-of-interest concerns, and his obvious biases are all challenges for journalists and all Americans. He creates the news, and when it's reported, he calls it fake. Regardless of his posturing and deceptive strategy of creating distractions and deflections of fact, he can't make the realities of his actions go away.

Trump's substandard, manipulative behavior and inaccurate, vile, and insulting rants are complemented by a descriptor frequently applied by him toward the watchdog media—lying. He has surpassed the Wizard of Oz because his intent seems far more divisive. He is not a communicator in the most basic sense of that word. His vocabulary is markedly deficient, and he consistently shows a lack of confidence and ability to speak extemporaneously when answering questions. In a sad attempt to appear more competent if only to himself, he habitually exaggerates with an omnipotent flair, but competency is not an outcome of these distractions.

Although the John Kelly appointment provided some hope for a change in this real-life *Animal House*[67] example of a White House, the constant that remains is Trump's needy, childlike, out-of-touch conduct so blatantly inappropriate for a leader of the US. He is not skipping through an enchanted poppy field as Dorothy and her gang did in the movie. He is trampling the country, its citizens, and important global alliances while not providing a level of confidence as he accomplishes little of meaningful benefit. Rather, he is inciting fear of what his id drives him to do that could have horrible consequences, and he most definitely showcases his lack of preparedness to address the country's important issues.

In consideration of your kindness, I take pleasure at this time in presenting you with a small token of our esteem and affection. And remember, my friend, that a heart is not judged by how much you love, but by how much you are loved by others.[63]

—Wizard to the Tin Man

Bullying is not an attribute aligned with kindness. The First Lady adopted childhood cyberbullying as a personal cause she wished to pursue. The president might want to have a talk with her to understand that Twitter is a common platform for cyberbullying, which he engages in with great aplomb. Or perhaps he already knows that. His tweets are rarely if ever constructive; they are more examples of his being deliberately critical in one way or another. Does the president have heart? He would be an anatomical wonder if he did not, of course, but it's only occasionally visible when it fulfills an attempt to gain a personal manipulative advantage.

As for you my friend, you are a victim of disorganized thinking. You are under the unfortunate delusion that simply because you run away from danger, you have no courage. You're confusing courage with wisdom.[63]

—Wizard to the Cowardly Lion

How prophetic. Trump may feel his statements and threats are exhibitions of courage, but his actions in no way demonstrate wisdom. He does act with no fear, but indeed, he should be fearful. Each day provides new evidence of his lack of qualifications for the position of president. "Enough!" will most likely become a cry of Americans; it's just a matter of time.

There is little evidence to support that Trump is organized

sufficiently to be the president of the country; instead, he is the proverbial loose cannon; he and the Cowardly Lion have that in common. The president confounds Congress, his staff, the media, and the world with out-of-the-atmosphere tweets and knee-jerks in his policy statements that frequently change with no clear and detailed legislative agenda. Instead, he presents only column headings of campaign promises. His bullish rhetoric, intimidating style, and know-it-all comments suggest someone as the Wizard pointed out who confuses courage and wisdom. There is little indication that his conclusions are comprehensibly based, filtered through the lens of history, researched, or the result of consultations with those who understand checks and balances wisely outlined by the founding fathers.

> *Therefore, by virtue of the authority vested in me by the Universitatus Committeeatum e plurbis unum, I hereby confer upon you the honorary degree of Th.D. Dr. of Thinkology!*[63]

—Wizard to the Scarecrow

An advanced degree would not help Trump in the same manner as the Scarecrow was helped once he felt he had a brain. It has been documented that Trump does not read in detail, including intelligence reports. Staffers reportedly provide a single page of bullet points on a topic Trump has difficulty speaking from while hugging himself but failing to deliver a cohesive message. When leaders of other countries are speaking, Trump is routinely inattentive, most often looking around, making facial gestures, mouthing words to someone in attendance, and generally showing little respect. A studied brain would help. Respect would help. Sensitivity would help. Intelligence would help. Giving up some of his television executive time would provide opportunities to read and study at any hour of the day or night.

A celebratory moment in the Wizard of Oz movie followed the realization that Dorothy's home had killed the Wicked Witch.

Ding-dong, the witch is dead! Which old witch? The wicked witch, Ding-dong, the wicked witch is dead.[64]

Dorothy was looking for a safe place over the rainbow; she just wanted to go home. The American people desire that place as well. Such a utopia is not ever totally achievable, but a sense of safety and security comes from having confidence in those elected to represent their wants and needs. Ego does not build confidence. Surrounding oneself with many Oz flying monkey reincarnations selected by the current administration reinforces the fantasy that "We know best, so trust us to fix all of what were the failures of multiple administrations past." Thus far, the reality Trump has created does not instill feelings of security or trust. Moreover, actions to date display woeful helplessness. Somewhere along the way and hopefully sometime soon, Trump will have an epiphany that flies in the face of his history on earth. Money will not block truth.

The citizens of our country have been set up. There is no rainbow, and Trump's fantasies are not the path to follow. Trump's house is coming unglued. Rats are deserting the ship as they are being discovered with greater frequency, and others who just want to remove themselves from the chaos are departing. History can document that full disclosure of every conversation and action in real time is not immediately shared with the American public by the country's leadership, nor should it be. Whether the reasons reflect national security concerns or because there are plans that take time to fall into place, these are not an affront to the public.

On the other hand, Trump and his staff have created a hollowness in trust, honesty, and candor. Lies have come to be expected, and further lies cover up previous lies. This scenario is a starting point of many discussions by the public and media. What does this say about the president and others? Is it any wonder Trump's approval ratings don't increase beyond his base as important leadership deficiencies continue to come to light because of his floundering approach to the office? Even mixing in a dose of common sense would help.

> *Perhaps it might be better, Mr. President, if you were more concerned with the American people, than with your image in the history books.*[68]

It doesn't take intense study to conclude that Trump is in the deep end of the pool and parades his clear incapacity to swim and lead this nation. His self-believed life preserver is losing air rapidly. If he continues in the same ways during his time in office, there is only one direction for Trump to travel in the pool, and it's not out. Drowning is a terrible thing particularly when you don't recognize it's happening to you.

The Wizard in the movie displayed more skills as a leader. Leadership is not bought; it is not an electable mandate from the people. Leadership comes from listening to others, respecting their experience, insights, and intelligence, and recognizing that sitting at a historic desk does not make one qualified for executing the responsibilities of a president or leading others.

Trump states that he has "spectacular" relationships with other world leaders when in reality it has become apparent that he has offended many of them in spectacular ways. It even appears he makes up statements in a grade-school attempt to impress someone. Former president Harry Truman had the famous "The buck stops here" plaque on his desk. Trump's golden emblazoned mantra is likely "I need no one."

Americans do not want more problems due to the person at the top of the executive branch and his advisers creating far more issues than they are resolving. Trump's false claims have reached mammoth proportions, but the result is not raucous laughter. Americans want reason, explanation, protection, and certainly a lack of fear at home and abroad. They don't want egos running amok and assaulting their lives. The public doesn't want to be suspicious that lies populate every statement and contribute to never-ending spin, making facts harder to torture out of these statements. Lies about fact only to make oneself look good are not appropriate. Slashing budgets and programs based on a bean-counting approach rather than change weighed against a determination of need is troublesome on many levels. The government is the largest business anyone has ever managed. Doing so does not welcome the same approach that may work in the private sector. Government management also includes the military and critical diplomatic relationships around the world, examination of national and international health issues, and education leadership that cannot be just a bone thrown to a campaign contributor.

Trump has stated unequivocally that he is not representing the globe but only the American people. What he does not understand or maybe just does not care about is that he is representing America to the world with his domestic actions and grossly adolescent and internationally impactful statements and policies. When does the winning he guaranteed begin? More important, compromise can be a win. Imagine that.

We are not in Munchkin Land. Making claims and stating policy that salves our wizard's id is happening at the expense of the American people. For now, the wizard is the proverbial bull in a china shop, but in Trump's case, it is not about just paying for the broken plates. Some would characterize him more as a wrecking ball swinging aimlessly and unconcerned with what is struck or who is hurt in the process or what long-term ramifications may result. He has continued to show he is light on knowledge and strong on hyperbole, and he makes little effort to become informed. Throwing experienced and informed people out of agencies or cutting budgets has no positive impact but instead frequently worsens perceived and real problems.

Dorothy tried to solve her biggest problem—how to return home—but to no avail. After her adventures with her friends and her foes, she was able to take a breath and refocus her thinking without all the clutter that had not allowed her to think clearly. Dorothy's simple solution has eluded Trump and his trusted advisers.

Trump appears not to be thinking clearly on most any topic as he personally creates the clutter with great vigor and acts with a single motivation—to be seen as tough minded—and of course he's always right. He makes statements that show his lack of depth, and he repeats the same words at every opportunity because he feels compelled to emphasize what he believes is important or what he remembers. And then he changes his mind and contradicts himself. His statements are all he has; light on content and heavy on absurd boasts.

He is making President Nixon's lack of truth telling seem insignificant. In the famous 1977 David Frost interviews with Nixon three years after his resignation, Nixon took a position that has been widely referenced: "When the president does it, that means it is not illegal."[69] Trump may find comfort in that statement, but he needs to look at its broader context. It is not a marching order for a president to not be transparent, though the likelihood someone will suggest that to him is very low, and Trump would not understand the context of Nixon's statement anyway. Trump should understand it's not okay to just do anything he wants. Nevertheless, though Nixon's lying set a high bar for certain, it is one that Trump is surpassing and has surpassed easily and frequently, and the truth bar is now so low that it is subterranean.

Credibility. If he continues to employ his threatening approach to domestic and international tests, Trump will come crumbling down even more quickly than what is already apparent. The Wizard of Oz had credibility with the people of Emerald City. To a degree, they complied out of fear, but Americans will not. What Americans fear is that they will be caught up in life-altering consequences because of Trump's bullying and know-it-all approach to every topic and situation. His international opponents will not jeopardize their own credibility with their citizens for Trump's sake.

Dorothy had a heart. The Wizard of Oz had compassion. We see neither of these characteristics in Trump. The day-to-day world of America's self-proclaimed wizard offers a daily menu of controversy, deception, deflections, distractions, and evidence of a hopeless inability to truly lead. He has shown himself to be deficient in so many ways that precipitating disorder grows each day and becomes his most notable attribute, but disorder is not a route to responsible change.

It's time for this wizard to get over himself and become a president. The tough guy and mentally flawed persona accompanied by a routine, condescending scowl, degrading gestures, and irresponsible statements have accomplished little. Even the Wizard of Oz, once revealed from behind the curtain, was more empathetic and real and showed himself capable of digesting needs and delivering resolutions. The president of our country is neither intended nor destined to be a figurehead just sitting behind the Resolute Desk. Rather, that person must lead and responsibly serve the country and all its citizens. Dorothy woke up from her dream to exclaim, "There's no place like home." The nightmare Trump is perpetuating on the US and the world continues, and our home is in turmoil.

Ding-dong.

Trump is sure to implode but hopefully not take the rest of the country with him.

> *It is not only for what we do that we are held responsible,*
> *but (also) for what we do not do.*[70]

CHAPTER 3

STRATEGY? WHAT STRATEGY?

All men can see these tactics whereby I conquer, but what none can see is the strategy out of which victory is evolved.[71]

—Sun Tzu

From the earliest indications of Donald Trump's interest in running for president to his glide down the escalator at Trump Tower in 2015 to punctuate his show-business announcement of his intention to run, there were seemingly endless alarm bells being sounded. A common theme that emerged was his overwhelming need to be perceived as the best, smartest, and so on because he genuinely believed he was all these things even if evidence portrayed far different conclusions. Being a legend in one's own mind is a heavy burden.

He demonstrated early on that he would not receive well any criticism, perhaps even constructive criticism, because after all, there was no one smarter in history. His opinions couldn't possibly be wrong, and those who said so were losers. Trump's reactions are very predictable. In speeches, press conferences, responses to media questions, in the presence of other world leaders, and of course his tweets, he has shown he is not the best or the smartest. Rather, his communication content provides insight into a troubled, boastful, untruthful, immature, and pathological soul. Trump has a burning need to be taken seriously as president, but his actions create the opposite effect. His approach to the office detracts from any possible positive view of his abilities or likelihood of success. He craves adoration but reveals little to admire. World leaders have quickly recognized that the way to Trump's heart and favor toward them is to praise him even when there is no reason to do so.

Long before the Republican primaries in 2016, Trump was a Reform Party candidate for president in 1987. He later registered as a Democrat and later as a Republican. He worked at showcasing his bravado, shouting claims with exaggerated, false, or no facts at all but shouting nevertheless. He wanted to present himself as knowledgeable as he manipulated public opinion and demonstrated strength. Was he serious? Did he have a plan for his future? Was it a plan he wanted to foist on Americans for his and his family's benefit? Were his actions just deceit personified? Could he develop a strategy to be elected president, or was he just led by his id? The answers to each of these wonderments may never be fully revealed.

He had no experience in government, so what was the point of his run for the presidency? How could he possibly be accepted by those with experience, or was his party simply fooled and overwhelmed? Did Republicans in 2015 believe they could solve the Trump problem by absolution—ignore him and he'd go away? As time passed, the country became more exposed to his increasingly absurd and outrageous declarations. The Republican Party began to witness a tear in the fabric of its conservative principles particularly among a cohort of hardline, anti-Democratic individuals.

The Republican primary debates witnessed Trump barking about his believed prowess on all topics, calling his opponents names, and in general demonstrating his lack of respect for nearly everyone in government and the private sector. His conviction that he was the personification of the best and brightest drove all manner of his insulting accusations about individuals and institutions. Then there were his rallies that at times seemed almost Hitleresque, and the Republican convention stage show. His contentious interactions with the media, except those he had carefully built relationships with over time such as Breitbart News and Fox News, grew and grew as his statements were challenged. Every controversial remark or action became an opportunity for him to create distractions rather than responsibly dealing with facts or substantively discussing issues of importance to the country. He routinely created deflections when his comments were shown to be in error or simply made up, but he did achieve without question a dominance of airtime and column inches.

Was this all a masterful, well-crafted strategy, or considering the ongoing controversies since he took office, just blind luck for Trump? Or perhaps it was a stratagem, cunningly schemed deception for his personal gain? What was occurring for certain was the making of an accidental president who was grossly inexperienced and lacked substantive plans for the country.

> *Now, therefore, I, Donald J. Trump, President of the United States of America, by virtue of the authority vested in me by the Constitution and the laws of the United States, do hereby proclaim January 20, 2017, as National Day of Patriotic Devotion, in order to strengthen our bonds to each other and to our*

country—and to renew the duties of Government to
the people.[72]

A nice thought for the day at his inauguration, but like many other examples of Trump proclamations, any bonds to each other and to our country have not been strengthened. The divisive history of the Trump presidency to date has weakened bonds, and the country is suffering.

Renew the duties of government to the people? The Trump proclamations miss the fact that the Constitution defines the duty and responsibility of government. It's that piece of parchment displayed with great reverence for all to appreciate in the National Archives down Pennsylvania Avenue from the White House. Trump may find it enlightening on many levels if he makes an educational field trip, no permission slip required.

Developing a strategy and successfully executing it impacts large numbers of people. Strategy constructed around an individual is the first indication that he or she will not consider the greater good. Meaningful outcomes from the tactics chosen for the strategy's implementation will be lacking.

Coming up with business and marketing strategies requires research, facts, and experience. Employing the right people with the experience and skills to develop an appropriate strategy is essential. Ignoring competitive business and product features, benefits, and advantages almost always assures failure. Measuring whether a strategy was correct and successful means evaluating it against specific objectives established at the outset. The objectives define the metrics and measurements set after the fact to prove that some erroneous outcomes are illegitimate. Those who jump to tactics without strategic measurable objectives find themselves unable to quantify success with meaning as opposed to stating outcomes that aren't based on facts.

Trump's political strategy is perhaps best described as bumbling by chaos. Trump has not substantiated that he has a plan about most anything much less a strategy to achieve it. What he does have is loud, often insensitive, consistently controversial, and generally offensive pronouncements. His statements commonly have no substance and are directed at a subsection of the population who respond to loud threats and lies that support their blanket opposition to Democrats. He points blame at everyone he chooses to denigrate and anything about which he could make an outrageous statement. He provides no indication that he understands the Constitution, the rule of law, or the process of working with Congress rather than alienating it. The exception of course is when he is mounting a defense for any attack on his personal and family business dealings, but in these instances, he most likely hands off to his attorneys and accountants rather than really studying the process or basis in law.

> *Strategy without tactics is the slowest route to victory.*
> *Tactics without strategy is the noise before defeat.*[71]

—Sun Tzu

Trump's tactics of shouting, tweeting, and insulting are not evidence of a strategy but instead these tactics are just noise and clutter that contribute to a divided country. His defeats have come in a variety of ways most of which he chooses not to acknowledge. The noise created drowns out any semblance of rational thought or planning. Because Trump won the nomination and election, it would be interesting to hear Sun Tzu's take on the outcome as Trump's focus was on a subset of the voting public; he lost the popular vote by a substantial margin. The Electoral College process handed him victory, but the motives of those making up that component of the election have yet to be fully explored objectively. Those in his campaign's inner circle and in his White House cannot anticipate what will be the next outrageous development. The only certainty is that that development will not be strategic or accompanied by objectives backed by rational tactical decisions. They are always ego driven, and the next crisis is always on deck.

Conceivably, he had no strategy other than relying on Electoral College support rather than on winning the popular vote. Was that a strategy or just an inheritance of partisan support? Most likely, Trump did not think he could be anything but the most popular candidate. He has shown that perhaps his most highly developed skill is generating knee-jerk reactions and tweets and keeping those around him confused about what he might do next. Some have suggested that this is just all show biz from Trump and that he knew exactly what he was doing during the campaign and since. That is a very hard position to substantiate, but of course, he will take the compliment as it strokes his narcissism.

Thus far, Trump has had little major legislative success other than his tax plan, which after many concessions finally passed Congress. Since its passing economists have pointed out consequences not receiving Trump braggadocio statements, particularly in terms of its growing negative impact on the deficit. Trump has attempted to fulfill campaign promises by undoing everything possible with executive orders most of which do not become implemented just because he signs them with his large black crayon. He gave no direction on health care beyond repeal and replace—mere accusations directed at President Obama. He continues to exhibit his biased approach to immigration only to find with each iteration of his biased bans that many are blocked or overturned by the courts. Yet in spite of his failures, he doesn't seem to learn anything from them. He changes position from one statement to the next tweet. This is not his intent of course, well maybe, but he just can't help himself. Trump doesn't have the ability to study and understand how to play well with others. Or perhaps he just doesn't care.

Accidents do happen, and the Trump campaign was emblematic of one accident after another. At every turn, amateurs on his staff were in a constant state of attempting to bail him out from an onslaught of controversial statements. Some of these people even today have the greatest job security of any occupation as his misspeaks keep coming.

Impulsive does not adequately describe the Trump approach to campaigning or the presidency, but the word does imply that his tactics during the campaign and since taking office are erratic at best. As he moved around his campaign playground, Trump rarely if ever had anything respectable to say about issues or his solutions. He criticized the opposition candidate, his own party, the media, and any opposition in view about what had or hadn't been done in the past. The most consistent claim was that only he could pull the country out of the morass he described with his repetitive claims. He campaigned on draining the swamp in Washington but has done little to describe the swamp or exactly what his prose meant. In his own clumsy way, he did foreshadow a swamp he subsequently has contributed to. Draining the swamp has morphed into a situation into which Trump is adding many more creepy-crawly things.

His ploy was seemingly to always be controversial, and those voters his remarks ostensibly impressed asked for no substance or proof of anything. Anything anti-Hillary was all they desired; his campaign was more of a sitcom striving to find a home in the Oval Office. Is this presidency just the on-air rehearsal for a forthcoming cable miniseries? Perhaps, or maybe it's just a private chess game Trump is playing out in front of the world.

The hardest thing about any political campaign is how to win without proving that you are unworthy of winning.[73]

—Adlai Stevenson

Chess is a game of strategy, but governing is no game, and approaching it as such may be Trump's downfall. Skilled chess players begin a game with a strategy in mind that slowly but definitely becomes apparent; they execute their strategies with tactical moves; they focus on getting their important pieces into position rather than simply pushing pawns. Trump spends a great deal of time treating everyone as pawns subject to his manipulations; his strategic endgame is never quite identified as his personal chessboard is frequently toppled.

By spending so much time with his pawns forgetting that moves by pawns can't be retracted, Trump creates situations in which any support they might offer are trapped in a state of dysfunction. Trump's pawn moves differ in that he uses them for verbal walk-backs, but once out of the game by his own ignorance or removal from his staff, they are rarely destined to become allies and instead become others' sources of help. The opponent in a chess games simply puts the pawns in his pocket.

How did Trump begin his game of becoming a candidate and getting elected? The end point of his chess game was where he started. He didn't have a plan to move to the center. He believed this was a game no one else had a right to play with him. He was so outrageous in his approach that he started in the center of the board by dominating all media coverage and out-shouting his opponents in the primaries. The plan was always to keep himself high in the ratings. He positioned himself as an expert in all things regardless of his lack of expertise and knowledge of the government. He worked hard to be seen as a self-proclaimed authority with the most superficial commentary on any subject, individual, the country, and the world.

In chess, controlling the center of the board is crucial, but in Trump's game, it is about owning it and removing any obstacles he perceives to be in his way such as Department of Justice personnel. His stumbling moves were not just about outmaneuvering his opponents but were also attempts to deceive the rest of us. He charged ahead with one contemptible move after another.

In chess, a single piece cannot alone work toward the desired outcome. On the other hand, Trump stands alone because he has repeatedly demonstrated that no one can manage much less control him. The other pieces on his board are not really supporting him as much as they are tolerating him and attempting to protect themselves. He desperately wants their loyalty, but can he expect that from people with consciences? Even his apparent demand that all on his staff sign nondisclosure agreements that would live for a period after his presidency demonstrates his need for control.

Solid chess strategy involves moving a piece to the best position while thinking ahead to the next move; the entire board and all pieces must be evaluated as components of that next-move equation. It is not about just one piece; it's a matter of offense and defense simultaneously, moving to the center of the board and blocking the opponent's attempts as well. Trump thinks that he deserves to be there; that is his starting point and maybe his end point as well. His brash, irresponsible moves are all defensive while offensive to the world. His personnel decisions are despicable and all about him at the center, and they are an imprudent means of shielding himself, he thinks, as the heat is turned up by the courts, special counsel, and the like.

While many are asking his supporters, "What were you thinking?" Trump continues his assault on democracy. Asking the question about what strategy he implemented during the campaign goes far beyond Secretary Clinton talking points and the running tirade of insults directed at all in his view. Once he was in office, what he perceived to be a legislative agenda sorely lacked any strategic approach for success that would include truly working with Congress. What he has termed an administration policy is much less than that. It's frightening to think the country's well-being and its place in the world is left to serendipity.

Chess is all about keeping your king safe, and without question, Trump is in sync with that strategy because he believes he is the ruler of his personal monarchy. However, his assumption is rough around the edges. As king of his domain, Trump expects and demands unending loyalty and most likely protection from all inside and external forces. Historically, Trump must have proclaimed himself to be a proponent of his particular golden rule—he who owns the gold makes the rules.[74] This rule first appeared in the Wizard of Id comic strip as the peasant followers ("idiots") responded to the autocratic king when told to follow the golden rule. Not surprisingly, Trump took that to heart, and he may demonstrate that on occasion, he did read personally influential material.

I hope Trump is learning that in governing the nation, he indeed does not make the rules no matter how hard he tries to or who or what he attempts to manipulate. But even as some of his moves are blocked or reality forces him and his staff to walk back from a tweet, Trump charges ahead with the next assertion from the growing Trump Repertory Theater. It's not strategic but simply Trumpspeak based on insecurity, falsehoods, and a previous lifestyle, but frankly, it's not good entertainment.

Another term in chess Trump clearly identifies with and speaks to involves moves that will threaten his opponents. Threatening may be what Trump does best—facts be damned. Clouding his past are threats of lawsuits, threats about government agencies, threats related to policies of past administrations, threats to members of his party, threats to allies, threats to leaders threatening the US and the world, and on and on. In his case, much of his threatening demeanor is senseless banter with no objective or meaningful purpose, and it frequently makes him look foolish. A component of a planned strategy? Perhaps, but most likely, it reflects only his ability to react via often incomprehensible tweets or with confusing responses to media questions. One can only imagine what it must sound like in the privacy of the Oval Office. Staffers must leave his presence rubbing their heads to clear the numbing invasion of their intellects.

When we consider how much time Trump apparently spends watching cable news every day and reacting to stories about him and throwing tweets into cyberspace, we see he had no strategic plan to help the country progress. His staff and attorneys are forced to understand that in spite of their direction and counsel, Trump is on his own. He trusts only himself. His inner circle is continually preparing for his next outrageous and potentially damaging moment. He has held live TV meetings in the White House with members of Congress or his cabinet that rarely accomplish anything beyond demonstrating his lack of knowledge in the face of those who take their responsibilities seriously and professionally.

The presidency dictates that those around the president are there for support, not to be fall guys for his shortcomings. Trump cannot allow himself to be seen as anything less than the smartest person in the room, but he doesn't have those credentials; no president does. Trump cannot be viewed as a stoic as that would be in direct contradiction to his every act and word. Following the philosophy of stoicism would mean Trump would need to be indifferent to pleasure or pain and show no emotion. He is driven by his delusions of greatness to the point of distracting himself and the country.

One thing is for certain—during the campaign and since taking office, he and his team have employed a reactionary strategy of addressing failures and controversy in the same manner. That's not really a strategy; it's damage control. Trump will tweet or say something that at times is just abject sensationalism that leaves all scratching their heads: "Did he just say that? Does he understand he just contradicted his previously stated position?" The result follows the denial, deflection, and distraction approach to the topic at hand. Trump takes out his anger on others and follows that with press briefings that reinforce the nonsense. On occasion, the spokesperson or guest commentator at a daily press briefing piles on more confusion. Media questions are deflected, answers are given that don't apply to the questions asked, and in some cases, questions from media representatives are simply ignored.

It eventually comes down to how he and his loyal staff manage crises, including those he has created. Successful crisis management is a matter of having a plan in place in advance particularly for situations that expose vulnerability, and with Trump, everything seems to expose his vulnerability. Nevertheless, certain components of a crisis management plan can be put in place, and one of critical importance is having a single point of contact for the media. For most administrations, the White House press secretary or perhaps the communications director would be that contact point, but in the Trump White House thus far, these individuals have not gained the media's or the public's trust. They have become behind-the-lectern puppets using pervasive Trumpspeak; they avoid giving insightful information and answers. Instead, the answers they give provoke more questions that are most frequently unanswered. To "help" their efforts, Trump often blindsides them with another provocative tweet. Adding to the confusion is the endless string of personal attorneys and official White House counsel appointees muddying the news with outrageous and confusing banter. Many of Trump's days involve something that requires crisis management that leads the news in terms of his relationship with Congress, Americans, and the rest of the world. Oh, and of course there are those crises relating to his personal issues.

Some crises are just problems that can easily be handled, but that is not the case for the Trump administration as his problems and larger crises are not predictable as they frequently result from his morning tweets. Something is always coming. Controversies occur with great frequency; once his tweets, comments, and actions are reported, the walk-backs from staffers just add to the confusion. If Trump would simply consider his behavior and remove his personal high bar of always being right, perhaps the constant, negative, unwanted attention he and his administration receive could be turned around, but the likelihood of that occurring is nil. Trump thrives on publicity and controversy, and if he harms someone, something, or a closely held belief of our democracy, so be it. His staff may not have considered how vulnerable he is because of his need for the spotlight, but these folks have become manipulative as well as they try to direct or refocus the spotlight.

Any crisis can cast an organization or individual in an unfavorable light. The risk is that the concerns of others become more intense along the way particularly if a crisis worsens because of action or inaction. Individuals and processes become scrutinized in many ways, some undesirable. Day-to-day activities become scrambled, and what might be normal in a sane world quickly becomes abnormal.

Trump and his associates have no normal. Every day seems to be a train wreck. The administration travels from a point of silence on an issue to a point of no return at warp speed. As president, Trump has the ethical responsibility of managing his never-ending crises whether or not he views them as such. In his case, his minimal governing ability has made matters worse. Trump does not grasp the importance of communicating clearly with all his audiences in terms of their wants and needs for information. He just continues to shout with greater frequency and volume.

He who establishes his argument by noise and command shows that his reason is weak.[75]

Trump has repeatedly stated that he doesn't want to say what his plans are whether he is talking about a conflict situation with a global ally or enemy or resolving a domestic issue. The problem here is that he takes that same approach with Congress. He has shown that his guidance on legislation is weak; he prefers to threaten or get on his personal merry-go-round that spins off confusion and constant changes in direction. This isn't a strategy but rather evidence of not really knowing what he wants to do as he hasn't taken the time to personally analyze information that could provide him some guidance. Even if he took that approach, there is nothing about his past to suggest he would follow that guidance.

Does Trump have a strategic approach to governing the country, or once again, is his strategy only to have all eyes and ears on himself? Trump does not have to provide any real effort to getting his name and face in front of the world as he does have black-belt skills when it comes to criticizing others while patting himself on the back. Only when it comes to keeping his name in full view often surrounded by controversy does he demonstrate consistency—but strategic thought? Hardly. Presidents are supposed to have and exhibit a grand strategy of some description and work diligently toward its execution. If making America great again is what Trump believes is his grand strategy, he is consistently falling short of anything resembling strategic planning. What is seen is random reactionism—bouncing from one bizarre thing to another—and random missteps.

He shouts about making America great and has become so emboldened by his base that strategy is really the last thing on his mind. Instead, he has taken bold steps that have provided the world with a sense that America has adopted an isolationist view as opposed to its historic and respected leadership position in the world. Pulling out of the internationally supported Paris Climate Accord, ending the Iran nuclear deal, and instituting trade tariffs that affected our allies and ultimately American citizens do not make America great again. He prefers to project a posture of dominance over allies, Congress, and the innocent.

Trump has shown his tendency to say one thing and do another. He buddies up to someone like President Xi Jinping of China and then turns around and raises tariffs and makes disparaging remarks about the leader. Strategic? When Xi, an accomplished strategic chess player, retaliates in some form, Trump acts surprised and threatens some more. Strategic? This type of behavior toward Xi, Japan prime minister Shinzō Abe, South Korea president Moon Jae-in, Canadian prime minister Justin Trudeau, and leaders in the European Union is sure to come due like a balloon loan in negative ways. In spite of what will be a disturbing wake-up call for America, Trump will look for someone else—anyone else—to blame and will accept no responsibility for what he has precipitated while America's stature and economy suffer.

Trump's immigration quagmire does not exhibit strategy at all because the foundation of his approach has been quicksand from his first attempts at banning immigrants from Muslim countries. He and his administration staffers failed miserably in the attempt to make sense of what Trump's suspicioned racist bias was attempting, and on more than one occasion, the courts blocked his actions. Trump has raised the concern of both political parties, evangelicals, and others who believe in human rights and dignity with his flip-flopping regarding the referral of individuals illegally crossing the border for criminal prosecution. This has led to the separation of children from parents, his zero-tolerance policy. Trump stated first that he would not sign any compromise bill put forth by Republicans in Congress. Hours later, he said he would sign a bill, but he followed that with conditions about DACA and border-wall funding. Others in his administration muddied the water further with contradictory statements that did not clarify and certainly did not reflect a coherent strategy. How does this make America great again?

Trump again has falsely claimed that Democrats in Congress are the root of the family separations that his administration was implementing. Fact-check: there is no such law. There is a law against improper entry and the Flores settlement,[76] which limits the number of days children can be held in immigration detention, but neither the law nor the Flores consent decree empowers the separation of children and their parents. Trump's decree is that "Democrats can fix their forced family breakup." The administration has made the issue remarkably partisan through comments from a variety of sources that say the "law" is about deterrence, stopping MS-13 gang members, and the like.

> The Democrats are forcing the breakup of families at the Border with their horrible and cruel legislative agenda. Any Immigration Bill MUST HAVE full funding for the Wall, end Catch & Release, Visa Lottery and Chain, and go to Merit Based Immigration. Go for it! WIN![77]

And then, Trump spins that separating children and parents is a form of deterrence for border security. How very compassionate. Trump is not interested in the threats these immigrants face in their countries. Are Americans noting how he is destroying the moral fiber of the country? If his strategy is to traumatize children to protect national security, is that what Americans have come to believe their president and country represent?

Does Trump have any understanding about what he is saying or doing on immigration topics and especially this one, or is he just focused on "winning" and poised to check a box for his base of supporters? There is not even implied sympathy at all coming from the White House, just a desire to win at all costs. Without question, there is also a marked lack of empathy as this quality does not seem to be in Trump's makeup. Some degree of empathy from Trump might produce positive outcomes that would speak for themselves. Trump has made his obsessive view of immigration so convoluted that negotiation and compromise are nearly impossible, and in the meantime, people and children are being hurt. Does he care?

He has faced resistance from the First Lady about the children separations as well as from a bipartisan group of former first ladies that includes Laura Bush, Rosalyn Carter, Michelle Obama, and Hillary Clinton. Each of these women is far more informed about the workings of government than Trump is because their husbands did not pursue the egotistical path Trump cares most about. If the late First Lady Barbara Bush were alive, her moral outrage alone against what Trump is allowing to happen to innocent immigrant children would provoke protest by American citizens "greater than ever seen before." The outrage continues to grow, and all that is missing is a human being to resolve the problem.

Trump boasts that only he can fix America, but on this issue and others, he passes the buck to Congress and turns his back on acting responsibly and compassionately. One has to look no further than Trump's impulsive actions on immigration fostered by his inciting his base under the guise of appearing strong to see his inability to strategize, plan, and work toward a comprehensive solution to a humanitarian problem.

In the corporate world, people who act without critical and strategic thinking, caring, and understanding and who cannot access and understand information are labeled as empty suits who don't last long. They have a lot of talk, supposedly good connections, and a well-polished ability to select good restaurants. In this case, the empty suit may well be the accidental president.

CHAPTER 4

PUBLIC RELATIONS—SPIN OR HYPE? MEASURING ETHICAL BEHAVIOR

Journalism is printing what someone else does not want printed: everything else is public relations.

—George Orwell

Orwell was prophetic when he wrote the above. Without question, Trump rebels against good and responsible journalism because his world focuses solely on what he says about himself, what he believes in the face of all evidence to the contrary, gratitude to others who are in agreement with his positions, and of course his need for adoration. Most assuredly, even when his own remarks are reported, he is unhappy. With this as his modus operandi, journalists face dilemmas; they want to print the truth, but when they do, Trump yells fake.

So according to Orwell, that leaves public relations as the blanket to cover everything else. Responsible public relations from the White House and Trump's supporters is the epitome of an oxymoron as releases from the White House are neither responsible nor professional public relations. Most often, those releases try to protect the president from himself or emphasize what Trump believes is most important and facts be damned. There is a marked difference between conscientious public relations activity versus an overwhelming need to never be seen in error on any matter and to cover up previous claims and misleading or false statements.

Professional and dedicated journalists work diligently in a world of facts, and if that means material appearing in print that Trump does not like, does it follow that those reports are fake? Does Trump make the leap that his social media tweets are true and trustworthy? Of course he does. Trump's tweets have been shown to be inaccurate and based solely on his need to be considered omnipotent. The Public Relations Society of America's operating principles and Code of Ethics for professional public relations practitioners do not support what many, including journalists, are inaccurately calling public relations. Trump is engaged in self-promotion at the highest level by thinking he can control what he wants printed. Hype.

So does the rhetorical question of public relations, spin, or hype have a single answer when it comes to the president? Most likely, an answer to that question would not please all parties, and depending on the respondents, the answers would potentially differ. The reason? What comes from Trump specifically and from his press secretary, attorneys, and others is rarely consistent as the topics change quickly but always with the goal of making it appear that Trump is never wrong. His handlers have had an increasingly difficult time crafting believable stories. It's also a matter of perception, not reality, that the White House is attempting to create with the public and the rest of the world. Whether creating this perception comes under a heading of spin or hype, the inconsistency of messaging makes the believability factor exceedingly low.

Doubt began the moment Trump entered his race for the Republican Party nomination for the 2016 election. Rants, shouts, insults, and lies became the norm, and after he took office, nothing changed. He has used his position in the style of a publicist promoting himself. His most trusted ally from history must be P. T. Barnum. Trump comes from a position of spin Trump-style with enough blowhard velocity to make one dizzy.

As he considered his presidential bid, he must have focused on I, me, mine in structuring his limited grammatical approach to the world. Any concept of representing the country and its citizens was missing as his statements were predominantly about himself. Saying that he is the greatest and continuously attempting to demonstrate that is not possible. Muhammad Ali was the greatest in his profession and a great communicator as well. Ali was legendary, but Trump's past, present, and future fall significantly short of greatness. Trump's attempts to represent the United States to the world have caused great concern among world leaders and our allies. His threats are largely empty, and he has surrounded himself with generally inexperienced advisers who at least visibly are not providing a positive impact as consultants or advisers for the well-being of the country. The personal agendas of some of his staffers are suspect as well.

Perhaps Trump and his staff could benefit from taking a short course in what are not characteristics of presidential behavior from a pure public relations perspective. His speech, his lack of empathy, and his intellectual deficiencies might benefit from an etiquette jump-start. So what makes one presidential?

Being elected president does not by itself make one strategically presidential. Standing with American flags does not make one presidential. Lacking the ability to speak and stay on point when desperately trying to assert perceived authority is not presidential. Threatening and bullying all those around you, including those who must execute a supposed legislative agenda, is not presidential. Telling the world at every opportunity how important one is, is not presidential.

Showing little respect or class in the simplest of social situations even with one's wife when politeness is all that is required is not presidential. Accusing others of lying while displaying a marked inability to tell the truth because personal vanity prevents it is not presidential. Showing unbounded narcissism and valuing oneself above all else is not presidential.

Encouraging outrageous behavior by advisers and staff in the form of inaccurate statements that are subsequently and quickly tweaked, defended, or denied in the guise of accuracy is not presidential. Using events that have intended reverent purposes to wail about oneself is not presidential.

Continually restating a position when the criticism of previous statements threatens one's ego is not presidential. Claiming nonexistent expertise is not presidential. Claiming superiority over far more experienced people is not presidential. Skirting rules, laws, traditions, and responsible behavior is not presidential. Finding or creating every opportunity to brag about oneself does not make one presidential. Attempting to manipulate others is not presidential. Boasting about achievements far beyond their value and significance is not presidential.

Voicing and tweeting continuous criticism about the previous president yet taking credit for the positive outcomes of that administration's programs is not presidential. Exaggerating, constant lying, and making false claims is not presidential.

Hyperbole is not presidential. A need to be in center ring in one's personal and family circus is not presidential.

Withholding information that will reveal true colors is not presidential. Cajoling members of one's political party to be in lockstep with one's opinions is not presidential. Creating controversy in the hope of convincing others how strong one is, is not presidential. Craving adoration, which leaders around the globe have determined is an effective means of manipulation, is not presidential.

Expecting full compliance by all to a stated position when facts clearly show errors in thinking is not presidential. Naming unqualified people with highly questionable ethics to high-ranking governmental positions is not presidential. And believing above all else that one is entitled is not presidential.

A strategic, detailed, and appropriately developed public relations plan to help Trump overcome all his challenges would be a career project for a professional. The president and many he has asked to join him in positions of importance demonstrate chaotic behavior that gives rise to real concerns for Americans and many around the world.

Trump should not attempt to characterize his ongoing misspeaks, false claims, and controversies as proof of his position. Characterizing outcomes that raise questions of ethics, constitutional affronts, lack of suitability for office, and investigations as partisan witch hunts are just other examples of distractions. Trump reinforces his personal insecurity in the face of pressure to the world with each tweet and ad-lib.

The election outcome showed that Trump had a substantial advantage in the Electoral College but that the popular vote was heavily in favor of Hillary Clinton. That was undisputable, or so it was thought. Following this outcome, Trump engaged in an ongoing tirade of tweets and challenges about millions of illegal voters. He followed that with arguments about the size of the crowd at his inauguration. What a way to start the presidency— whining about a victory and the size of a crowd. The turnout to his inauguration showed he was not the most popular person he wants to believe he is. So to hype his importance, he started a verbal war that probably had the opposite effect. In no one's public relations handbook would such behavior be recommended for any president.

Trump spends considerable time rehashing topics about matters he feels are important though no one but he clearly cares about them. Why are they so important to him? Even Trump's inaugural address demonstrated that his speechwriters attempted to use symbolism as a means of inspiration, but his remarks came across as very dark and notably uninspiring. He even chose to motivate the country on his first day in office with the phrase, "This American carnage stops right here and stops right now."[78] That must have made everyone proud to be an American.

The speech also fell short in execution thanks to Trump's delivery. He was so used to saying anything that floated into his mind that advance preparation was an uncommon demand on him. He went as far as to say later that it had not rained during his speech when real-time coverage showed rain beading up on his overcoat and on the ponchos worn by those around him on the platform. That was not the beginning of his baffling statements of course, but what did he hope to gain with such ignorance and a refusal to accept an obvious and simple reality?

Trump's bravado and condescending style get in the way of clear messaging. He over-promises and thus far has shown he is quite adept at under-delivering. Even the Wizard of Oz had more skill, but he and Trump have the common characteristic of making false statements. Both wizards fooled their constituencies, but in Trump's case, his constituency is catching on to his deceptions.

Trump's unchecked lack of tact was evident in his sweeping criticism of the US intelligence community. The day following his inauguration, he destroyed what could have been a fence-mending moment with the CIA. This was a real public relations opportunity for him to recognize those who had demonstrated their dedication to democracy and love for their country in the ultimate way. When he was standing in front of the agency's Memorial Wall, he strummed his vocal cords about the dishonest media and the crowd size at the inauguration. Dreadfully sad. He insulted the agency, its employees, and most important, those who had died serving the country.

The Women's March on Washington took place the same day similar marches in this country and abroad did. They collectively demonstrated that Trump was being questioned as a viable president; the marchers wanted to give voice to many other issues justifiably important to women and men. And Trump's take? He chose to take it as another personal criticism, another unfair sortie directed at his ego. Once again, he deflected attention from the purpose of the march. "Why didn't these people vote?" he tweeted.

Why? It's impossible to determine how many of the marchers voted, but it is safe to say that with Trump losing the popular vote by such a large margin (right—the illegal voter claims), it is fair to assume that a majority of those people who were eligible to vote in this country had done so. He overlooked the fact that even those present who were ineligible to vote were there because the issues they were airing were important to them.

In case another fact eluded him, the march was not US-centric. Those participating in marches in countries around the world did not vote in the US election. Well, perhaps Trump can confirm that if he checks that statement with President Putin of Russia. These global marches showed that Trump had not fooled the world and was recognized for what he believes about himself.

If there were any in his camp who were concerned about his image, where were they? It was too early in his administration for staffers to be hiding or resigning, but his reaction to the Women's March was an early indication that he would not seek advice before tweeting as a president, not as an outspoken candidate. His demand to be considered the world's greatest authority about everything was just beginning to come out. Those on his staff with insight would have said, "Let me out of here" and updated their resumes immediately.

In spite of Trump's wanting to continually relive the election and criticize his opponent, the comments he rolled out were more of what was in his memory bank when he couldn't figure what else to say about topics that had nothing to do with the election.

Trump pulls out his go-to hoax, witch-hunt, and fake-news cards to deflect what he perceives as negative attention on himself and from what he is complaining about, including the special counsel investigation. He missed the concept and understanding that saying less can mean more. His inability to let things go just makes what are already bad situations for him much worse. It crushes his ego.

Methinks thou dost protest too much.[79]

If he would use the time he wastes stroking his ego to accomplish things for the country and strive to be a respected president, the outcomes might be considerably better.

Trump's claims, defense attempts, and spin further illustrate his egotistical flair, show the world how irrational and unpopular he is, and reinforce concerns on many levels. His knee-jerk and hip-shooting reaction to almost everything threatens sane discourse. When all else fails and he cannot come up with anything substantial to say, he plays the Clinton email card, lack of an adequate DOJ investigation of her—"Where's the server?" "No collusion," and so on. Name-calling endears him only to those following him off the cliff like lemmings. Any public relations professional attempting to establish a solid image for Trump would resign the account as any such campaign would require a cooperating client.

Trump became president under circumstances that remain in debate, and until he vacates the position by the will of the people, the DOJ, or Congress, he resides in the Oval Office. Trump is no longer intimidating his hotel employees, attorneys, accountants, contractors, his family, and others to do his bidding in the private sector. Or do we know that for certain? Then and now, he is subject to laws and the Constitution. Using smoke and mirrors to skirt what is in place to protect all Americans may ultimately be only one factor that could trip him up as he attempts to use those basic tenets of our democracy for his personal gain.

Manipulation will not work as people are watching—many more than he would like—and they are not necessarily fans of the chaos he creates. He attempts to avoid accountability, protect his family and income, and disguise his past and current behaviors, while deflecting attention away from events and actions that reveal his lack of credibility. Such actions may well be the precipitating components of problematic outcomes. Everything he says or does is subject to examination, not blind acceptance. His maneuvering will be challenged, and the truth will be exposed. More than the eyes of a few attorneys and accountants will be looking in depth at his actions as now the examiners will include Congress and the DOJ.

He is routinely spinning most everything and taking verbal actions he shouldn't. If he listened to his never-ending list of personal attorneys and followed what might be a legal crisis-management scenario, he might lessen the ongoing damage. The problem of course is that he denies ever doing anything wrong.

Although firm conclusions are not yet available regarding possible Russian election collusion with the Trump campaign, some areas of investigation may move from suspicion to proof, others may result in charges of obstruction of justice, and others could be dismissed. Suspicions about Trump's ethics discrepancies, past financial dealings with Russia, and others' claims may substantiate troublesome aspects of his personal life to everyone.

The special counsel is conducting a professional investigation, and in the process raised many questions as many topics and individuals are pursued. Trump has responded by criticizing the special counsel and the process in general and demanded that the investigation be shut down. In spite of his maneuverings, Americans, Congress, and the media are watching.

Before and since his election, Trump has complimented Russia's Putin. In spite of great concern expressed by many and questions related to why this has been the case in view of Putin's criticism of the US and his actions around the world, their bromance is indeed startling. Trump held off implementing approved sanctions against Russia for some time and has gone as far as to congratulate Putin on his reelection though the world recognizes that Putin's election had not been a democratic process. The late Senator John McCain commented immediately after Trump's congratulatory remarks, "An American president does not lead the free world by congratulating dictators on winning sham elections."[80]

Trump has not commented negatively on what is widely believed to be a Putin-approved poisoning of a former Russian spy in the UK, but he did join several European countries in expelling Russians as a solidarity move and certainly his most stringent response to Russia. He later became upset as he felt he had expelled "too many" Russian diplomats compared to other countries. Such situations do nothing to support Trump as a leader who understands elements of diplomacy and further, in this case, do not distance him from Putin and Russian connections.

Whatever the extent of Russian involvement in attempting to influence the outcome of Trump's election, it is not the first time Russia has tried to do so. In the early days of the Cold War, the USSR premier Nikita Khrushchev was quoted as saying, "We can influence the American election"[81] in reference to candidates John Kennedy and Richard Nixon. Social media and other technological developments apparently became Russia's primary tools for meddling in the 2016 election, and according to the intelligence community, the meddling is ongoing.

Since what some might describe as his fateful inauguration day, the Trump presidency has demonstrated a lack of support for or even appreciation of the US system of government. Those defending Trump using highly developed skills of political spin feed his apparent objective and need for creating controversy. However, these insiders appear not to have had any positive influence in an effort to tamp down the Trump mystique. Trump rolls on through a string of false claims, deflections to avoid direct accountability, and distractions that at best serve to embarrass the country internationally and impede progress domestically. With no sign that Trump will behave responsibly, his defenders must question their motivations. If not, all reason must have escaped them.

Much has been written about Trump's characteristics in thought and action compared to those explored in George Orwell's novel *1984*.[82] No argument here, and a reread of William Golding's *Lord of the Flies*[83] may also be in order. (Perhaps a good bedtime story for Trump.) A *Lord of the Flies* review described the novel as allegorical. The author presented the conflict between civilization and savagery that developed between the novel's two main characters—Ralph, who represents order and leadership, and

Jack, who represents savagery and the desire for power. Which character best describes Trump historically and now? No, not whom he might aspire to be, but how he sees himself.

Trump has mounted a new bully pulpit. President Theodore Roosevelt coined this phrase with the positive intent of providing a forum or opportunity to state his opinions and be listened to concerning his agenda and vision for the country—public relations. He was also the first president to recognize the importance of public opinion, and in effect, without its being named as such, he created the daily press briefing. Trump on the other hand appears to have stopped reading for facts early in his education or conceivably never read history at all. He has taken an adversarial approach with the media and anyone he feels opposes him, which is distinctly different from his predecessor's and most rational human beings' approach. It is natural not to agree with everything in the press, but Trump doesn't seem to understand that news can still be accurate and that the media could even be an ally on some subjects. Thus far, Trump has given the media little to be positive about in its reporting, but that lack of positivity does not mean stories are universally inaccurate because he does not believe them or does not want them told.

Trump's number one tactic is acting like a petulant child who has just had his favorite toy taken away. He whines and moans but doesn't understand why the toy was taken away. It's really not an act with Trump; it's just the way he is. His responses to legitimate questions show how little he has to say even while not employing mental edits to make his comments more appropriate and coherent.

The world is very concerned about North Korean leader Kim Jong-un's rantings and unbridled behavior that it fears could result in a nuclear holocaust. Trump has consistently stated he would never telegraph plans to an enemy; when asked about Kim's threats, his response was, "We'll handle North Korea, it will be handled. We handle everything."[84] Is Trump really qualified to and capable of making life-altering decisions for the country? Handling North Korea is a decidedly empty statement for those justifiably concerned. Of course, Trump and Kim applaud themselves at every opportunity.

If the summit that took place between the two produced any significant positives, applause may be appropriate, but at this stage, the signed agreement provided little else than a photo opportunity for both parties. Did Trump learn boisterous distraction skills from Kim or vice versa? Either way, they represent two potentially out-of-control individuals who momentarily are acting as good friends. Even with what appear to be positive developments between North and South Korea, the world thus far has not been privy to the backstory. We must view with some trepidation such a dramatic altering of North Korea's decades-long rhetoric and action.

North Korea has countered the Trump administration's arrogance by stating that its intention to denuclearize, unveiled at a historic inter-Korean summit, was not the result of US-led sanctions and pressure, and it warned the United States not to mislead public opinion.[85] The Trump administration essentially ignored this revealing statement. There is far too much history with North Korea to accept that Trump's threats were the precipitating factor for the meeting. Another curtain has yet to be pulled back, and what may be found could be far different from the utopian comments Trump offered following the meeting with Kim.

> Just landed - a long trip, but everybody can now feel much safer than the day I took office. There is no longer a Nuclear Threat from North Korea. Meeting with Kim Jong Un was an interesting and

very positive experience. North Korea has great potential for the future![86]

Of the four major actions outlined in the postmeeting joint statement, one spoke to the topic of denuclearization: "Reaffirming the April 27, 2018 Panmunjom Declaration, the DPRK commits to work toward complete denuclearization of the Korean Peninsula."[87] Important words to consider in this statement are *work toward*. There is nothing about these words that provide the guarantee Trump boasted about. True, Kim blew up a few buildings as a distraction, but no intelligence suggests that negatively affected the country's nuclear capability. Instead, what has come out since the meeting is that Kim is updating and upgrading North Korea's nuclear capability. This hardly supports the Trump postmeeting boast.

Trump's approach to communication is to shout out unsubstantiated accusations and criticism of the media. He also criticizes respected individuals, including his cabinet appointees. He misuses information, makes up his own sources to support his frequently outrageous claims, routinely turns to very old news and complaints, and repeats them in the most inappropriate forums (e.g., interjecting a politically filled rant to a gathering of nearly forty thousand Boy Scouts in July 2017). Other presidents speaking to this annual gathering focused on good citizenship, serving others, and having common bonds and ideals. Whom did Trump think he was addressing as he launched into another reliving of the election and criticism of many? Are these types of verbal outings in any way presidential and good public relations? Trump's spins are so easily questioned that it seems he just likes seeing his name in lights.

The president needs to consider his relationship with the country, Congress, the media, and the global community, not just his tried-and-true 40-plus percent base. Any discussion or negotiation must have a win-win goal. All parties will experience pain of some nature in reaching an outcome, but what is evident thus far is that Trump feels he must win for himself at every turn and render any opposition submissive to his will. He is not building a golf course, casino, or hotel and in the process intimidating contractors. This is our country; in spite of the pedestal he puts himself on, he is accountable to us all.

Trump and his administration have created a multitude of uncomfortable situations. The ongoing inappropriateness of Trump's tweets, official nonanswers to questions, and ongoing leaks of information create more of the media coverage he objects to. Trump chooses not to follow his advisers' direction and thus precipitates ongoing chaos. His choices do not show any semblance of strategic thought or planning. He and others have put Sarah Huckabee Sanders in quicksand in terms of her credibility with the media and the American public. Press secretaries are linked to their own brand of spin, but the goal, as envisioned by President Theodore Roosevelt, was to create a dialogue with the media and put forth a president's responsible and truthful narrative. The disconnect comes when what began as a platform for truth becomes something far less. In this administration, spin has been irreparably linked to lies, and there is no sign that will change.

Each day brings more false and misleading statements. As of October 30, 2018, according to the *Washington Post,* Trump has made 6,420 false and misleading statements in 649 days in office—over nine such claims daily.[88] Trump's and his administration's attempts to correct or modify these false and misleading statements and address challenges by the media and others frequently result in their sinking further into the morass of distrust. That scenario fosters the opinion that all public relations statements are lies, a stigma that dismisses responsible public relations campaigns that serve important outcomes in, say, public health education. Indicting a respectable profession couldn't be more incorrect, but there is no denying that Trump's administration's spin is far from factual, professional, or respectful public relations.

The possibility of aligning Trump's actions with reasonable and ethical choices is remote. There is no telling what he believes; his impulsiveness leads him to one misstep and misstatement after another. Conscientious ethics provide a road map for all behavior and generate trust, honesty, and integrity—the basis of truthful communications. However, whatever he believes, his actions and words are not always ethical.

Ethical behavior and personal integrity put an individual in a positive light, but that light fades when one or both are lost, and they are nearly impossible to regain. Life's challenges require a personal ethics audit before any action is taken. Long-term consequences must be considered so society is not harmed. A lack of qualifications presents other challenges that can negatively affect quality thinking, accuracy, and judgment, and what may be legal isn't always ethical.

Questions of ethics are not exclusively the property of modern society. If Trump were to consider historically developed approaches to ethics and followed one form or another of ethical behavior, others would have a basis for attempting to understand his words and actions. Aristotle recognized that following moral absolutes is difficult to sustain, so he proposed the golden mean—finding a position of ethical balance between two extremes (excess on one end and deficiency on the other); that would put one on the path of acting morally. For Trump, determining the extremes is relatively easy but not necessarily productive; he repeatedly shows that any degree of balance is impossible. His life features one type of excess after another, and his deficiencies reveal themselves continually; he is swinging like a pendulum rather than resting in a state of balance.

Immanuel Kant postulated the moral philosophy of the categorical imperative—the idea that we should make ethical decisions as if they could become universal laws. Someone tempted to lie to the media to prevent embarrassment should consider the consequences of lying becoming a universal law.

John Rawls's theory of social justice advocated for decision makers to put on a veil of ignorance—look at a situation from all points of view—but that is not Trump's strength or method. Every situation is about him and his opinion alone, so only his viewpoint is required. That does not provide reassurance for the country in spite of all his promises.

Philosopher John Stuart Mill advocated for all decisions being directed at producing the greatest good for greatest number of people—utilitarianism. Leaders of the United States should not argue against this approach, which would of course include defending the Constitution. Trump could put aside his idiosyncrasies and his only-about-me thinking and try to learn about the responsibilities of the presidency. But under him, the presidency has deteriorated; his actions are viewed with great apprehension. What can possibly be trusted about Trump with ethics as a valid yardstick? Where is the evidence that he guides himself with a universal rather than a highly personal and flawed sense of ethics? Any administration from the top down must demonstrate established values and ethics.

What values are Trump and his administration following and demonstrating through their communications and actions? Are there values at all or just examples of the bad behavior he and his staff engage in because they don't know how to act responsibly?

- autocratic paranoia

- neediness
- lying
- encouraging violence
- uninformed decisions
- questionable hiring practices
- lack of transparency
- antagonism
- threats
- questionable morals
- support of dictatorial global governments
- allegations of possible collusion with an enemy of the United States
- assigning blame to anyone not in agreement with the president

These (and this list could go on) do not form the basis of a productive and ethical presidency.

Trump's continual fast-and-loose play with facts and the diversions he creates are counterproductive. His actions and those of his staff, counselors, and family are subject to scrutiny. If the facts don't support his position, he habitually makes up his own version of a situation. He has created remarkable false distractions in the form of questionable family involvement (or not) in inappropriate foreign situations, separation from Trump family business interests, chaos of his insider staff, resignations, firings, and insulting world leaders along the way. Distractions are not complements to responsible governing.

Chief counselor Kellyanne Conway generated little credibility with the media and others who listened to her; her style telegraphed that spin was always what lay ahead. By speaking rapidly from an ever-changing but memorized script and providing deflective responses to media questions with monotone delivery, she showcases her amazing support for Trump. She is the spinmeister for Trump and defends his actions with consistent flair. Like her employer, she does not accept the possibility she could be wrong about anything. Enter alternative facts. The Public Relations Society of America (PRSA) was quick to issue a rebuke of that term, and it stated the public relations professionals' approach to the dissemination of information and the ethical reasons and principles for not misrepresenting this information.[89] Truth and perhaps a study of the PRSA Code of Ethics would help all Trump's mouthpieces. What was not widely discussed was that the PRSA statement was tangentially recognizing Conway as a public relations professional, which is difficult to substantiate.

When faced with suspicions and ongoing investigations of himself and associates without as yet incontrovertible proof, Trump and his spokespersons invoke plausible deniability; they deny any knowledge of or responsibility for others' bad behavior. Without proof beyond a reasonable doubt, denying and in some instances lying provide shelter of some sort, but a special prosecutor or congressional intelligence committees might still uncover the truth. At least one of these committees has fortunately not accepted blatant partisan behavior as an objective. Trump may well have lost sight of truth altogether.

Plausible deniability is a good friend of some politicians; it's the go-to tactic to provide wiggle room. For Trump, it's a way of life. He has a talent for pretending he hasn't said things that others have documented well. He has weaponized this approach and exploits it frequently to cloud the positions of those who oppose him and disguise truth in the eyes of his supporters. During his campaign for office and as president, Trump has run right up to the line of doing or having done something that is difficult to justify or explain, but he always leaves himself an out—plausible deniability. Many of his supporters apparently don't make the distinction or care to.

Trump does not understand that continuing to deny and default to contemptible tweets and bizarre statements does nothing to build respect for him or his administration. He has accomplished little, and he has no easily quantifiable plan to address any of the country's pressing issues. Granted, some of the things he tries to speak about push forward the Republican Party agenda. He spins out a headline most frequently in the context of criticizing Democrats in Congress or about the election process. On these occasions, his spin lacks details and substantiation. His businessman's approach to running the country involves leaving it to others to understand a topic and speak cerebrally about it rather than bothering to study the matter personally.

When others question him about one statement or another, out comes the fake-news deflection because he does not have the facts to provide a reasonable response. On the other hand, a reasonable response is not necessarily his goal. The president overlooks the fact that his confrontational approach has less and less meaning even for his base. There is little substance in his responses because he speaks in only very limited ways. Off camera, it may be different, but based on reports from those who have left his staff and others who remain and leak anecdotes of his behavior, it is not a stretch to conclude that his rhetoric is quite impossible to manage and takes up significant space and oxygen in the White House.

Unlike the Cowardly Lion, Trump does not exhibit a lack of courage, but it is often horribly misplaced. He is a vindictive vigilante attacking anyone questioning whether he has been truthful or has acted appropriately in the past or present; he draws more attention to himself in the process. He likes that, of course, but that raises further questions about the created crisis of the moment. His responses further erode his credibility. Even if he were inclined to seek public relations help in building an image worthy of a president, as long as those around him are speaking to an audience of one, the likelihood of change is nonexistent.

Trump and his staff are highly skilled at hype and spin, but a carefully developed public relations program does not exist, as that would require examples of positivity, not a never-ending defense of mistakes. A change in personal style is most likely not even discussed because Trump will be Trump. That much is certain and unfortunate.

CHAPTER 5

THE CHILD WITHIN

I have found the enemy and he is me.[90]

Donald Trump acts like a child. He is frequently rude, inappropriate, insulting, and overbearing, and he demonstrates his disapproval of most anything crossing his personal radar and with great frequency later contradicts his previous statements. His most common tactic is twisting, ignoring, or stretching facts to a point of disbelief by most yet believable by him, all with great ease and commonly to the point of an adult tantrum. Often, there is no basis at all for things he says or tweets. His style is domineering with ongoing strings of false claims that a variety of audiences, including Congress, the DOJ, White House staffers, and of course the media recognize.

Trump is patently naive about the government and its institutions and deficient in essential knowledge a president requires to govern appropriately and efficiently; he has no ability to work at a level of understanding that could make him more respectable. The similarities to a child attempting to get his way are disturbing.

He is not a leader at his personal White House playground, where chaos reigns. His antics and demands are tolerated as a "peacemaking" defense by others. He is not leading the country, his party, or a strong legislative agenda. He is not acting as a leader period. His exploits embarrass this country. Former secretary of state Colin Powell said, "Great leaders are almost always great simplifiers, who can cut through argument, debate and doubt to offer a solution everybody can understand."[91] This clearly is not a description of Trump, who does not strive to understand the topic at hand. Trump is unsophisticated in this regard; he precipitates arguments and debates even among his allies, and he focuses on what is wrong with everything. His attempts at compliments in weak moments are empty and lack empathy. He does not offer comprehensive solutions, just boasts and headlines. Obviously, Secretary Powell was describing someone else.

Recess is Trump's standard. He jets around the country and the world shouting how great he is. He considers those who don't agree with that position as being simply in the way. Playing highly qualified people against one another as a means of shielding himself from his own ineptitude is all he knows; the White House bully struggles to demonstrate any presidential characteristics. At best, he is acting out as most children do at times, and the unfortunate, ill-timed, and inappropriate role he is playing is that of an accidental president. The accident is not about votes but instead about his landing on the ballot at all.

Trump piles papers on his Oval Office desk as props for photo opportunities, but from his statements, it is impossible to think he actually reads them. Perhaps that is too strong. He undoubtedly reads at least some summaries prepared for him, but informed opinion is not forged from bullet points. In-depth, daily intelligence briefings have reportedly gone by the wayside. They may represent an interference with his "executive time," watching television/cable news outlets to gain fodder for his tweets. His lack of patience has been documented, his boredom with learning has come out with great frequency, and as publicized by reports filtering out from his staff, his attention span is apparently on a par with a child having to be repeatedly told not to do something.

The turnover of his staff and those serving in important advisory positions has been astonishing when one considers the reasons for the turnover. Some will make reasonable comparisons to other administrations in this regard, but they most often simply state numbers and percentages. They do not consider the circumstances for the departures from Trump's administration as controversy reigns supreme. Trump has fewer and fewer potential players on his bench to come into the game, and those few who remain will not have splinters from excessive bench warming. Even some of Trump's outside lawyer draft choices have turned down his invitations to join his personal legal team of defenders.

Handling an adult's childish behavior is a challenge and particularly so if that person is the president. The sales pitch directed to join the Trump administration must be quite a creative exercise, and apparently, it is losing its efficacy. Qualified candidates are turning their backs while Trump assembles a group of controversial yes-men and yes-women while much of the country watches in horror, disbelief, and concern.

His responses to media questions, embellishments of remarks prepared for him, and his tweets illustrate that this child is not a communicator. What he demonstrates is boastful commentary and narcissistic needs. Consider these statements from his early Twitter repertoire leading up to his nomination:

Nobody but Donald Trump will save Israel. You are wasting your time with these politicians and political clowns. Best![92]

Nobody would fight harder for free speech than me but why taunt, over and over again, in order to provoke possible death to audiences. DUMB![93]

Nobody understands politicians like I do – all talk and no action. They will never get our country where it needs to be, truly great again![94]

I hope all workers demand that their @Teamsters reps endorse Donald J. Trump. Nobody knows jobs like I do! Don't let them sell you out.[95]

Wow, just saw an ad – Cruz is lying on so many levels. There is nobody more against Obamacare than me, will repeal and replace.[96]

No one has done more for people with disabilities than me. I have spent many millions of dollars to help our-(*sic*) and am happy to have done so.[97]

Nobody will protect our Nation like Donald J. Trump. Our military will be greatly strengthened, and our borders will be strong.[98]

The media is so after me on women. Wow, this is a tough business. Nobody has more respect for women than Donald Trump![99]

Nobody beats me on National Security[100]

The economy is bad and getting worse-almost ZERO growth this quarter. Nobody can beat me on the economy (and jobs). MAKE AMERICA GREAT AGAIN.[101]

Are these comments appropriate for a president? Such conceited remarks have not and will not bear fruit; they foreshadowed what the country is experiencing today, and that is not expertise in the subjects of his tweets. Some offer the defense that these tweets were just part of the campaign, that everybody running for office becomes boastful, but consider his tweets after he took office. No doubt it is disconcerting for Trump to have to prove himself, as he has never had his back to the wall on such a stage. He is the poster boy for speaking without thinking, and he misses the concept that claims are just claims until proven, but for certain, they are distractions and deflections.

Reading can present a challenge of sorts to him, and understanding what he reads could be his biggest hurdle. When reading from a teleprompter, he gives the appearance of a child onstage for a first recital. Nervous. Apprehensive. "Let me out of here." Those who have coached him to speak softly and slowly when addressing important audiences—not at his rallies, where he is outwardly uncontrollable—apparently believe this approach can present a picture of a more empathetic president. The reality is that this coaching, if it actually occurs, makes it ever more apparent that he is not empathetic at all. And when he goes off the teleprompter material, the hyperbole flows and flows to the point of inducing nausea for some and praise from others. Believability remains an issue.

As an example, in an effort to put more pressure on North Korea, he stated,

> I do want to say because people have asked, North Korea, we imposed today the heaviest sanctions ever imposed on a country before. And frankly, hopefully, something positive can happen. We will see. Hopefully something positive can happen. But that just was announced, and I wanted to let you know ... We have imposed the heaviest sanctions ever imposed.[102]

Here are the prepared remarks he was to deliver:

> Today I am announcing that we are launching the largest-ever set of new sanctions on the North Korean regime. The Treasury Department will soon be taking new action to further cut off sources of revenue and fuel that the regime uses to fund its nuclear program and sustain its military by targeting 56 vessels, shipping companies, and trade businesses that are assisting North Korea in evading sanctions.[103]

Decide for yourself which approach is informative and based on searchable facts.

Speaking extemporaneously is not a skill Trump exhibits. The outcome at such times most often falls short of being clear communication and showcases his struggle. He is repetitive to a fault, and the more he speaks, the worse his statements become. His words defy him, but of course, he must not recognize or understand that. He is a child who breaks something but denies doing so in spite of the evidence.

Hyperbole definitely resides in Trump's repertoire of skills; there had to be one. Unfortunately, this skill does not communicate knowledge or command respect. He has even touted this approach as a reason for his successful dealmaking.[104] His favorite word is *very*; he thinks repeating it make his statements stronger.

His approach reminds me of the dialogue between Emperor Joseph II of Austria and Mozart in the movie *Amadeus*; the emperor suggests to Mozart that his opera had too many notes: "My dear fellow, there are in fact only so many notes the ear can hear in the course of an evening."[105] Too many words, Mr. President.

His tendency is to frequently use the phrase *a lot* normally as a placeholder for a word or phrase he doesn't access easily from his memory, but these words contribute little. He will not go down in history as any threat to the legacy of President Ronald Reagan as the great communicator.

It's a mess is his go-to phrase for assigning blame for anything to anyone but himself. Trump's reasoning commands that one ignore his failed appointments, resignations, firings, minimal legislative success, and so on and cast blame in any other direction.

Incredible is the adjective he uses in all references to his staff or appointees (e.g., "doing an incredible job") and frequently when he describes how badly Democrats or his party have dropped the ball (e.g., "acted incredibly poorly on repealing Obamacare"). This word has even become a favorite of the current press secretary.

I can tell you is the phrase he uses after criticizing someone or something as if to say he is expert on the matter. Most often, he delivers this phrase in a condescending fashion coupled with a facial smirk or rolling of his eyes.

Believe me is another self-endorsement of his intellect and knowledge. Really? It's *incredibly* hard to believe him *a lot* when he is creating such a *mess, I can tell you.*

Greater than the world has ever seen. These words from the wizard miss the point that he is clearly describing the dysfunction he is causing.

I'll be honest with you means that he has a revealing point to make and that he will do so truthfully. Interesting concept.

Intelligent and experienced people greatly appreciate the fact that Trump does not attempt to speak in a foreign language in any diplomatic situation because it is beyond difficult to understand his points in English. Those translating his comments into other languages have a significant task. English idioms do not always translate well, and much less does Trumpspeak, and mistranslations can unintentionally offend those of other cultures.

His limited vocabulary and disconnected thoughts render his communications exceedingly difficult to understand, and repetition doesn't help. Perhaps he should be pitied. It is easy to threaten and bully with expletive-laced statements as he may have used in his business dealings, but that does not suit a president or his country. Regardless, on occasion he has not hesitated to use derogatory language and profanity.

His propensity for using social media as a presidential communication tool defies logic. He may think it is an easier means through which he can express himself, but again, reality enters the picture. Remember covfefe? This is the reference that he applied to the condition of the country that baffled all. The world is confronted with a sarcastic, vile, and insulting trail of tweets that embarrass the country. No one has to seek his tweets because the media and other outlets report them with great frequency, ridicule, and shame.

The recent doubling of available Twitter characters provided him only more opportunities to misspell words, destroy grammar, and ramble on about disjointed topics as he attempts to demonstrate he is the greatest authority on any subject. As a child would, he brags about his millions of followers on Twitter as evidence of his support. Unfortunately, he forgets that millions of his followers are simply waiting for the next outrageous tweet for comic relief. Regrettably, his tweets are also on display for millions worldwide and repeatedly demonstrate that his communication skills are lacking. What would happen if Twitter suspended operations for a month? Let's make that happen and see if we can't get the country focused on real progress.

Implying that media grossly understated and manipulated news of the inaugural turnout served no purpose; he was a child acting out, and he ultimately forced others to degrade their reputations in support of this needless whimper. Sigmund Freud would have loved to have had such an obvious case study of his model of the psyche.[106] An in-depth review of Freud's model would be too much here, but here's a summary of it.

The id reflects the instinctual trends—boasts, lies, narcissism—Trump displays. The superego mirrors what parents have taught and is internalized as cultural rules. It is hard to imagine that his parents taught him his behavior—"grabbing them by the p———." The ego is the traffic cop that can halt the id's behavior. Trump's psyche is a flagrant representation of a short circuit between his neurons and the synapses that connect them; it's impossible for him to control his instinctual needs. He uses no filters or traditional broadcast seven-second delays before delivering his next pronouncement.

Trump is driven by his id. Based on his business dealings, his derogatory behavior toward and comments to the other Republican candidates during the primaries, and his criticism of the Democratic Party candidates and the sitting president, it's obvious he does not care about others or their opinions—only himself. Here are a few samples from before and during his campaign:

Sorry losers and haters but my I.Q. is one of the highest - and you all know it! Please don't feel so stupid or insecure, it's not your fault.[107]

I will be the best by far in fighting terror. I'm the only one that was right from the beginning, now Lyin' Ted and others are copying me.[108]

I will be the greatest job-producing president in American history.[109]

I am the BEST builder, just look at what I've built. Hillary can't build. Republicans can't build. They don't have a clue.[110]

I am attracting the biggest crowds, by far, and the best poll numbers, also by far. Much of the media is totally dishonest. So sad![111]

I have proven to be far more correct about terrorism than anybody- and it's not even close. Hopefully AZ and UT will be voting for me today![112]

I have been drawing very big and enthusiastic crowds, but the media refuses to show or discuss them. Something very big is happening![113]

What did he expect to gain by these self-absorbed, braggadocio statements? The size of his inauguration crowd? Why would that topic be necessary? When Trump opened the door to this silly controversy, comparisons were made to his further embarrassment. The media reported his claims with unbelievable tongue-in-cheek composure. Trump just couldn't get past the fact that he was not perfect and that he could be wrong. The numbers don't really matter no matter who is estimating them. Photographic records were clear, but the president chose to be personally offended. It must have been a conspiracy against him!

He created the inauguration-crowd firestorm due to his need to be the biggest, first, and best. His statements, the then press secretary's chastising of the media, and the chief counselor's propensity to spin, deflect, and defend her boss in the face of facts set the stage for distrust of anything coming from the administration. It established a negative culture from the beginning, and it has only increased, not subsided. Trump makes comparisons constantly on many subjects albeit most clearly inaccurate and of little importance.

During the campaign, Trump's personal physician, Harold Bornstein, MD, provided a one-page letter that included this statement about Trump: "If elected, Mr. Trump, I can state unequivocally, will be the healthiest individual ever elected to the presidency."[114] This and other over-the-top language in the letter is not common in a physician's evaluation summary, and it raised suspicions. Later, Dr. Bornstein said Trump had dictated the letter.[115] The first official physical examination for Trump as president was conducted and reported by the White House physician, Dr. Ronny L. Jackson, who stated that Trump's overall health was excellent. According to Jackson, Trump asked that a mental component to the exam be included, and Jackson administered the Montreal Cognitive Assessment[116] test as part of the examination. It's a preliminary tool used to identify early dementia or cognitive impairment but does not constitute an extensive mental examination. Jackson reported that Trump managed a perfect score on the assessment test, and to no one's surprise, Trump touted his score on social media.

Some have questioned how competent Trump is even to the

point of questioning his stability and cognitive functionality. Some have called for a specific and medically sound mental evaluation, and some clinicians even banded together after Trump's first year in office to suggest outwardly that he was an unfit president.[117] Without a face-to-face evaluation, this claim is inappropriate, but it is nevertheless concerning as Trump presents himself in a daily display of symptomatology that align with more than one psychiatric disorder. The suggestion that Trump undergo a sound evaluation is not unreasonable. At minimum, many feel there is reason for concern, but again, a professional, in-person examination is the only true means of making a credible diagnosis.

An examination of diagnostic criteria as stated in the American *Psychiatric Association Diagnostic and Statistical Manual–V (DSM-V)*,[118] which was published in 1952 and frequently updated to reflect subsequent research, is recognized worldwide as an invaluable tool for the medical profession. The *DSM-V* is a proven reference to assist physicians in making a differential diagnosis from a patient's presenting symptoms. The category of psychotic disorders includes symptoms such as delusions—fixed beliefs resistant to change even in view of conflicting evidence. Feelings of persecution such as a belief the person will be harmed or harassed by others and a grandiose outlook characterized by a belief the person has exceptional abilities, wealth, or fame are included.

Symptoms of one form of a psychotic disorder can include disorganized thinking or speech demonstrated by switching from one topic to a totally unrelated topic. Answers to questions may be obliquely or completely unrelated, and speech does not show effective communication.

According to the manual, symptoms of paranoia include a pattern of distrust and suspicion that others' motives are based on ill will or hatred for the individual. A borderline personality disorder is characterized by instability in interpersonal relationships, an elevated self-image, and marked impulsivity. One gathering of symptoms that cannot be easily put aside is narcissism, grandiosity, a need for admiration, and a lack of empathy.

This brief academic examination of mental health symptoms is not a diagnosis of Trump's mental state; all that can be rather authoritatively said is that Trump could be considered a troubled man in some ways perhaps because of his struggle with the reality that he was elected president. He is defiant on so many levels that he shows no allegiance to authority, only to himself, and blames others for his mistakes. He tweets seemingly to disturb if not outright annoy others. Are these the traits of a president who has the interests of the country as a tantamount guiding principle and an objective of his position?

What is the purpose for the outrageous and divisive events he brings to the country and the world? Making a claim that he is unhinged remains unsubstantiated. To answer why he acts the way he does commands that logic be applied, that civility be considered, that ethics be understood and respected, and that it should be tacitly recognized that the outcome of his behaviors are observable. He is playing with people's lives and the country's institutions owing to his need for constant adoration that seemingly guides every tweet and a belief that his every word has great meaning. His words do have meaning, but they most often rip the patriotic and organizational tapestry that has made this country celebrated and respected. His actions also provide clues for those who have an agenda to destroy America with a perfect and potentially easily manipulated target.

The president rambles on in his discourse with himself much like a child fantasizing himself in a variety of superhero roles. The statements emanating from Trump's soul show that the vitriol and lies have little logic or end. His decisions are most often emotional and impulsive and raise concerns among rational people who suggest that without firm checks on his childish ways, the country might be drawn into any number of detrimental scenarios domestically and internationally. Through attempts to show his bravado, Trump thinks in only the short-term, but as Winston Churchill advised, "Never engage in a battle of wits with an unarmed man." Trump should take that to heart as it may be the way his opponents at home and abroad view him, and if so, his decisions could create long-term problems for America.

Trump needs to think about how childishly he presents himself. He should remember that he just can't take his ball and go home as a child might do when challenged. The country is not his ball.

CHAPTER 6

CRONIES, THE WEAK, THE LOST, AND THE FAMILY

In looking for people to hire, you look for three qualities: integrity, intelligence and energy. And if they don't have the first, the other two will kill you.

—Warren Buffett

Integrity is an admirable characteristic in anyone, and coupled with honesty and unquestionable ethics and moral values, it provides a foundation for living and working responsibly. Trump demonstrates for the world that these foundational characteristics have not been included as an historical basis for Trump's life. He has created quite a different image of himself.

In 2016, Americans "hired" Trump in spite of his frequently questioned integrity. He played out his somewhat predictable behavior during the primaries and in particular in the debates with other potential Republican candidates, during the campaign, and now daily as president.

With few exceptions, it seems integrity was not on the list of hiring criteria for the White House transition team and staff. Perhaps it's a quality Trump doesn't understand or care about. He ignored President Obama's advice about not hiring retired army general Michael Flynn as his national security adviser. Did he think that was some sort of Democrat trick? Trump often repeated his claim during the campaign that "I knew more than the generals" and apparently in addition, he placed no value on the experience and insight of an outgoing president. Was it too hard for him to accept the advice of someone who knew what the position of national security adviser required and what the presidency required?

More to the point, if he knew more than the generals did, why did he hire Flynn? The rebuff of President Obama's advice was soon to come back and haunt Trump as Flynn was in place for less than a month before resigning because of the investigation into Russian tampering in the election and subsequently for Flynn's other personal interactions with Russia and for lying to the vice president. Flynn later admitted that he had earlier lied to the FBI, and it is yet to be fully understood after cutting a plea deal with the special counsel just how much additional information Flynn has since provided. The collusion investigation may unearth other insights into Flynn's actions and Trump's campaign.

Flynn was just the first to leave the administration. The personnel revolving door at the White House during Trump's first year was spinning, and that was depressing for the country because in many cases, the replacements have turned out to be somewhat stained themselves. The administration's inefficiency and lack of transparency was and is unrelenting. The travesty for the country is that the personnel departures have continued and that stability is only a concept, not a reality, in the Trump White House.

Others nominated for key posts, including cabinet positions, have withdrawn from consideration for service some because of issues in their backgrounds and perhaps others because as time and controversies occurred with alarming frequency, the prospect of being associated with Trump was not attractive.

Trump must have believed that after a successful run, he would be omnipotent. He equated the leadership of the most powerful country in the world with how he managed his real estate business. How could he not be a great president? From what we know about his business dealings, they may not have foreshadowed success as a president. His ah-ha moment on election night when it became clear he would defeat Clinton must have scared him almost to death. He had won the game but had to face the fact that he did not know how to be president or where to begin. The boasting about his abilities to win was over.

Given what transpired in his first year in office, Trump seems to have identified that his knowledge void was deep and that he did not bring the necessary awareness, demeanor, temperament, or interpersonal skills to the presidency. He had to have realized one hopes that his perception of power was inaccurate. Since taking office, he has contributed little to the country beyond destroying the foundation of what makes the country great. He must understand that the control he wants is not the degree of control he can achieve.

Hiring people is not to be undertaken lightly in the private sector or in government. Trump's management style is quite difficult to nail down. Like someone on a teeter-totter, he has zigged and zagged from one side of a topic to the other, and the selection of staff members has been stalled in the process. Nevertheless, without question, his style or impulses contribute to hiring decisions whether they are informed or not. Personnel decisions he has made or blessed have repeatedly demonstrated that no one has thoroughly vetted all candidates for positions on his staff. It is difficult to assess Trump's input as he ping-pongs his own understanding from day to day, hour to hour, even minute to minute of what a job might entail. He thus puts himself in a position of not making informed decisions; rather, they are consistently impulsive and emotional. Those around him may make suggestions and argue internally, but in the end, he creates controversy on Twitter about people, and he makes announcements often to the surprise of his staff. Perhaps in these instances, these are not decisions at all. Instead, brain neurons fired, and what he spoke or tweeted was not filtered much less based on facts. Trump cannot be accused of having policies; his Trumpian objectives are shifting targets, and thus, it is easy to imagine his hiring criteria are constantly in flux as well with the exception of his demand for undying loyalty. In the case of his family members' appointments, qualifications didn't matter at all.

Trump's apparent belief in an autocratic approach to governing suggests he feels entitled to absolute governmental and personal power. In spite of his lack of constitutional knowledge, he operates as if he knew all he needed to know. The presidency and the White House immediately took on the appearance of a handball game being played with a Super Ball,[119] and integrity and honesty picked up speed and went rapidly downhill from there. Each day brought more bounces to Trump's plaything presidency that produced more and more rises and falls due to his impulsivity, false claims, and manipulations of facts and people.

He appointed and hired a gaggle of people who were inexperienced in the ways of Washington, DC, and governing; in some cases, they lacked respectable ethics and responsible past behavior. Many of his cabinet nominations also followed this path of nominating individuals unqualified for their positions. In some cases, his actions and selections baffled many, and that made prospects for the future look ragged at best. His antagonistic interpersonal skills eroded any possibility of his forging beneficial relationships with the Democrats. Power struggles ensued in the White House, and he stifled cooperation even with his party's leaders. His inability to work across party lines always led to his blaming the Democrats for most everything while in fact the divisions among his party's members were increasing and shredding cooperation as well.

Holding a position in the Trump administration may have looked to many like an opportunity to serve the country, an admirable objective. But for many, their time in the White House became or has become embarrassing; they consider their time spent in the Trump administration as something they would like to omit from their resumes—"What have I done to my career?" There has been speculation that following the 2018 midterm elections, many staffers will jump ship regardless of the outcome. They will consider their time with Trump as a definite negative mark on their careers.

The dysfunctional Trump administration must be a prime example of what Peter Drucker was referring to when he wrote, "So much of what we call management consists of making it difficult for people to work."[120] He was referring to the business environment, but his assessment certainly applies to the Trump White House as well. Trump makes it difficult for everyone, but it's a challenge to determine if he is managing at all. It's not a matter of musical chairs in the White House because only Trump hears the music. If the music were ever made clearer, aides and staffers would be better off not sitting down at all and instead quickly look for the closest exit.

The initial cast of protagonists Trump put in his inner circle at the White House included some who had worked on his campaign but had no experience in government service. They matched Trump in that respect, and he may have decided that was a good balance, but they did not nor do they today constitute an ideal group of advisers on which the country should depend.

It does make one wonder how Trump and his inner circle arrived at his subsequent hiring list. Were there others outside the White House giving advice and supporting particular candidates? Was Trump leading or being led? As time passed, it appeared that some whom Trump thought he could trust and depend on were pushing his decisions in concert with their highly biased beliefs. What no one was controlling was Trump's pointless tweets and his overwhelming need to be the boss.

To his initial group of staff and advisers, Trump added his daughter Ivanka and son-in-law Jared Kushner—nepotism of the highest order. What was he thinking? Were they subject to thorough vetting? They had no experience in government but were true family insiders he could trust to watch his back. Perhaps. Over time, however, those two outwardly demonstrated little in the way of serving the country productively, provided a string of embarrassing moments, and in the case of Jared Kushner, became one of the subjects related to the Russia collusion investigation.

Kushner's financial dealings prior to and during his time in the White House continue to be examined. As the special counsel's work continues, other topics related to Trump, including how other countries could have viewed Kushner as a high-value target close to Trump and who could be manipulated to their advantage, are under examination.

It serves no purpose to list all the hirings, firings, and resignations thus far in the Trump presidency, but it has been reported that after his first year, Trump had more than a 40 percent staff turnover.[121] Add to that number numerous people who have declined the opportunity to serve him, those who resigned from the Department of Justice, and others who have recused themselves from any role in the investigation of Trump's alleged involvement with the Russians during the campaign and after his inauguration. This long list is more evidence of his lack of ability to vet or make sure others vet his hires. If that had been Trump's actual practice and his direction to his staff, he may well have nominated or appointed qualified individuals, but by all appearances, Trump is adept at ignoring all advice, keeping his staff in the dark, and routinely surprising all with his personnel announcements.

One of Trump's earliest attempts at appearing important was his signing an executive order regarding ethics and his appointments.[122] That order required that every appointee on or after January 20, 2017, must sign an ethics pledge that stated,

> As a condition and in consideration, of my employment in the United States Government in an appointee position invested with the public trust, I commit myself to the following obligations, which I understand are binding on me and are enforceable under law.

It's worthwhile to consider Section 1, paragraph 8 of this pledge: "I agree that any hiring or other employment decisions I make will be based on the candidate's qualifications, competence, and experience." This is certainly reasonable, but Trump has obviously exempted himself from this pledge; his steady stream of flawed appointments are apparently frequently based on his whims and those who say what he wants to hear, including how wonderful he is.

Some of the Trump administration positions such as cabinet secretaries require Senate confirmation as do ambassadors and independent agency heads. Some of his nominees were confirmed, but there have been a number of instances of inappropriate behavior, including extravagant spending and inappropriate personal expenses incurred, that have been far outside the bounds of the positions' authority.

The number of government positions unfilled at this point is quite remarkable. He took sixteen months to nominate someone for the ambassadorship to South Korea, a geopolitical hotspot to say the least. Was that another case of his staff's ineptitude, or was it because the importance of the position was lost on him?

Trump of course blames all the unapproved positions on the Democrats, which couldn't be further from reality. Some have suggested that both parties are being very careful deliberating Trump's nominations considering the person at the helm of government. On the other hand, consider some of those confirmed nominations and controversies surrounding them that have surfaced later.

Is the lack of qualified people wanting to serve in a Trump administration a significant issue related to accepting the criteria of Trump's noted loyalty and nondisclosure demands? Maybe it's just the mystic handshake requirement.

Early on, Trump said that there were too many people in government jobs and that he didn't want to fill all those jobs. However, many posts are essential, not unnecessary. What Trump and his inexperienced staff may have overlooked is that those appointed to acting positions do not have an endless pass from the nomination and confirmation process. A law passed by Congress in 1998[123] prevents an administration from overstepping its bounds regarding Senate confirmations. An incoming president has three hundred days to fill these positions, and the impact of not meeting that deadline, which Trump has certainly not met, can be a source of trouble. If someone in an acting position after that period makes an unpopular or incorrect decision, it can be challenged in the courts as improper. Someone needs to be watching the store, but clearly, it may not be the president or his staff. Worse, the law is apparently just being ignored out of ignorance. Congress, where are you?

During the primaries and the campaign, Trump shouted to the world that his business acumen would mean progress for the country "greater than the world has ever seen before." One would assume that evaluative hiring decisions based on required criteria and qualifications would be one element a successful businessman would bring to the presidency.

Another example of his supposed business acumen the country might have expected to benefit from was his management abilities. Any successful business leader will be quick to agree there are different management styles that will breed success, but what Trump has exhibited isn't one of them. Different situations require different management approaches. A president may shift management styles as circumstances dictate, but one overriding constant is required—the president must command respect not by demanding it but by earning it, and Trump has not done that. Americans continue to be taken aback at the statements he makes, the profanity he uses in open settings, and the name-calling he directs at his staff and cabinet members; he referred to Attorney General Jeff Sessions as the cartoon character Mr. Magoo.[124] Trump apparently cannot stomach being shown to be incorrect or accept that reasonable and rational people will not jump off the cliff with him hand in hand. A study of the Mr. Magoo mystique would reveal to Trump that the character was certain of what he thought he was seeing even though he was incorrect. Another potential moment of learning for the president.

For many, the knee-jerk reaction to answering the question about Trump's management style is that he demonstrates the characteristics of an autocratic dictator. This is a top-down approach with primary commands given that evidence a pattern that communicates, "This is your job—Do what I say or you're out" on all social and political issues. Thus, where employees may be operating daily based on fear of losing their positions, Trump has spent far more effort in threatening than firing. It is difficult to know if Trump's staff is truly empowered. Is his staff allowed to provide alternative recommendations? Is the Trump hierarchy so structured that only the most trusted person has his ear? Does Trump internalize information provided at all, or does he react only to the last thing he heard on Fox News? He contradicts himself day to day and at times with greater frequency than that.

A critical downside of autocratic managers is that those below them allow them to do it all. Those allowing this type of environment to occur frequently have an agenda they're pursuing in the background. Innovation goes by the wayside, and a collaborative work environment suffers greatly. The ongoing infighting and power struggles in the White House could certainly be representative of an autocracy with the bonus of having little in the way of true intellectual guidance from Trump.

Alternatively, a bottom-up management style is one that encourages feedback from those on the organizational chart before decisions are made, even relatively simple ones, and this style has the potential of creating more camaraderie. Subordinates are freer to express concerns without fear of repercussions, but in this environment, those under the leader have little power even though more of the staff may feel involved. Still, in a top-down situation—and here again, Trump might feel he is actually establishing an environment that encourages input; involvement seems to most predominately come from family and those he feels are unquestionably loyal to him and in lockstep with all his decisions, but such people are frequently undercut.

Trump seemingly doesn't attempt to actually persuade those around him or intellectually bring them to the reasons that influence his impulsive view of a situation or action he feels needs to be taken. Forming consensus opinion on an issue may never occur as a result. He frequently surprises his inner circle by changing positions and advocating steps that do not resemble prior conversations or conclusions. Is he a persuasive manager or just an out-of-control and frequently irrational one?

If there was any evidence Trump managed by a majority-rule approach, citizens might take some comfort in that. Instead, he shows that most often, he is not interested in others endorsing his position; what he most clearly communicates is that he always knows best, and that becomes the root of his decisions. Besides, the word *majority* probably gives him a decided twitch and reminds him of the lost popular vote.

Is he a hands-off manager? He certainly wants to give the appearance that he is in control, but his overwhelming need to control has not endeared him to others, including his staff, generals, diplomats, senators, representatives, and many others. On the other hand, some of the White House staff may view him only as a reality TV personality and thus think staying out of his way is their personal best policy. Even the likelihood of Trump providing clear direction is a difficult expectation for his cast of characters, and that does of course contribute to his need for control. His speeches frequently have errors because he goes off script, exaggerates, twists data, and makes false claims. There is little evidence that he prepares his remarks himself, but what does that say about the staff members who write them? It is obvious which tweets he personally cobbles together versus those written by someone else in damage-control mode when clear communication is required.

Is there a management style that best describes Trump's approach? Of course—management by chaos, which most certainly he would deny, but Trump has gone on record saying

CRONIES, THE WEAK, THE LOST, AND THE FAMILY

that he likes conflict, so is it possible to say he has indeed accomplished something postinauguration? Conflict abounds in his administration. The Jeb Bush "chaos president" reference[15] has rung true. Attempts at giving the impression that Trump delegates tasks and policy to far more qualified and informed insiders is indeed only that—an impression. His ever-changing statements create chaos for his staff, Congress, and the public. He is an enabler of disorder. Whether it's too many Diet Cokes, too much television, too much golf, or too few insights, Trump's style is nonproductive, confusing, uninformed, and yes, chaotic.

From the beginning, those who wished to be considered for a position in the Trump administration were swayed by the distinction, not by the reality of what price they might pay in their careers and perhaps their sanity. Job descriptions were not apparent, and even if they had been, Trump's style would precipitate the distinct possibility of the descriptions and responsibilities changing on a whim. Doors have opened and closed for individuals in the Trump administration, and with only familial exceptions, there are no locks on the door. Multiple individuals have served in the same position over the first year (e.g., communications director, press secretary, national security adviser, chief of staff, etc.), and those who have lasted the longest must be operating on an endorphin high. Even the most recent chief of staff, John Kelly, joked that leaving his post as secretary of Homeland Security and coming to work at the White House was the result of "doing something wrong and God punished me."[125] Humor can be a good coping mechanism. Even more recently, Kelly volunteered in an interview that the White House was a miserable place to work.[126]

Trump has created one of the more visible presidencies in the history of the United States with a special prosecutor and the media being the most vigilant in attempting to discover and understand where Trump has come from and where he might be headed. The announcement that Supreme Court Justice Anthony Kennedy was retiring caused immediate concern about whom Trump's replacement nominee might be. The Senate majority leader mandated that the nominee, Brett Kavanaugh, would be confirmed prior to the 2018 midterm elections. That mandate was indeed accomplished, but not without considerable controversy surrounding Justice Kavanaugh and the confirmation process. Elections are looming (always), and currently, these seem to be the overwhelming focus and concern of Republican Party leaders and donors. Trump exudes confidence that Republicans will remain in power in Congress, and creating the Supreme Court in his image is for many a disturbing consequence.

Thus far, in spite of his boasts, Trump's greatest achievements are more about how not to guide the ship, hire the crew, and avoid the storms. His need for control is illustrated by his need to have more-direct reports than good management would ever dictate. Style? During an interview on Fox News, he was questioned about his personnel vacancies in his administration, particularly in the State Department. He said,

> Let me tell you—the one that matters is me. I'm the only one that matters because when it comes to it, that's what the policy is going to be. You've seen that, and you've seen it strongly.[127]

Yet another incredulous statement about his greatness. What matters is putting competence as a primary qualification for a position right below integrity and how the right people in his administration just might help him accomplish more than photo ops. He just doesn't get it.

CHAPTER 7

INEPTITUDE ON STEROIDS

The difference between stupidity and genius is that genius has its limits.

—Albert Einstein

What's in store for the United States today, tomorrow, several Trump-dominated years from now? Trump has withdrawn from the Paris Climate Accord and thinks it can be renegotiated. It can't. He has withdrawn the US from the Iran Nuclear Deal and thinks sanctions will make a difference. Iran announced that it intended to negotiate staying in the deal with European countries, Russia, and China. Trump has taken total credit for the summit with North Korea because of his pressure tactics and threats. North Korea issued a statement that expressed this was inaccurate and suggested he not mislead the public.[128] Each of these examples has the potential for long-term negative consequences, but Trump is interested only in claiming wins; he forgets he is just as likely to lose as there are no guarantees in negotiations or misguided boasting. Add to these concerns the seemingly always out-of-touch misleading shouts about domestic issues.

The country and the majority of its citizens are being dragged into an abyss of lies, suspicions of Trump's personal and family financial gain, a deterioration of essential global relationships, a self-serving belief of what is ethical behavior, childish threats leveled at any individual or entity that opposes him, and a belief in his success far greater than what fact and truth reveal. Perhaps special counsel Robert Mueller and his staff will make the great reveal with facts before Trump has tarnished democracy in the US even further, deteriorated relationships around the globe, and demonstrated to his base of supporters that he is only manipulating them.

Trump is at the head of this march to gross failure and is showing no evidence he is a leader. He was elected by partisan politics through the votes in the Electoral College and allegedly supported in some fashion by Russian meddling in the election in unprecedented ways. In spite of the findings of the country's intelligence agencies and sanctions that Congress approved against Russia because of the evidence, Trump continues to somewhat suspiciously support Russia. As recently as June 2018 Trump deflected the Russia meddling topic again.

> Russia continues to say they had nothing to do with Meddling in our Election! Where is the DNC Server, and why didn't Shady James Comey and the now disgraced FBI agents take and closely examine it? Why isn't Hillary/Russia being looked at? So many questions, so much corruption![129]

He has stated unequivocally that he believes Putin, who has said there was no Russia meddling in the election. And nineteen months postelection, he is still attempting to direct a narrative that is positive about Putin in spite of the evidence all the while being critical of others. Being so out of touch with reality is not comforting. If this is not a reason for a reevaluation of his position, it makes one think there is more to be learned.

Since Trump has taken office, truth has been in a state of steady decline as it pertains to him and others in his administration. Daily lies from the administration have become even more frequent. When challenged by the media about an absence of facts and his contradictory statements, Trump declares reporting as fake as if to say that responsible and ethical journalists have written the words he has spoken. The result is more attacks and new lies, deflections, and distractions.

The president is governing through his convoluted musings and with a disregard for the Constitution's meaning and purpose. He is taking credit for all manner of things he has had nothing to do with during his first year in office. His tweets resemble a rewind of *Fox and Friends* programming. Trump provides nothing that inspires confidence in his intellect or abilities beyond well-practiced and repetitive but empty boasts. Giving someone the benefit of the doubt as he or she establishes a reasonable approach to new leadership is admirable. With Trump, however, the result has been a continuation of the behaviors witnessed as he entered the presidential race, and before.

The country has witnessed his many shortcomings, inappropriate behaviors, and offensive language; he lacks the commendable qualities and abilities to be in office. His base resists admitting his leadership deficiencies, which raises the question of how they are attracted to each other in spite of the ongoing controversies he generates. As Trump took office, even his most vocal opponents hoped for this president to be successful. After all, it was their country at stake too beyond ideological differences.

Unfortunately, Trump bases success solely on his personal wins some of which may turn into significant losses for the country. His base stands strongly behind him as Armageddon approaches.

Polls have measured people's confidence in Trump's capabilities and progress. His strong voter base continues to overlook his many misgivings; the overwhelming number of his messages is intended only for those individuals and the values they represent. His endorsements of special-election Republican candidates have not had the effect he thought they would have. Undoubtedly, he realizes his persona is not as influential or immediate as he thinks. His most frequent achievements confuse, alienate, and amaze those who are more informed, experienced, and responsible. The difficulties with his staff and leaks, which of course he blames on the media, are simply symptoms of a crippling disease, and all the distractions he creates do nothing to cure it.

Does Trump command respect for his intelligence? No. He has difficulty reading, speaking extemporaneously, or demonstrating any expertise on subjects beyond financial matters, which of course are near and dear to his soul, but his predictions are routinely awkwardly embellished and exaggerated. Going on record that he did not need to prepare for the meeting with North Korea's Kim is yet another glimpse of how powerful he views himself. What he touts in his rantings as fact frequently betray truth. He is a TV-focused president; conscientious preparation and studying for understanding evade him. He attempts to appear authoritative but instead demonstrates he has little understanding of important nuances of legislation, diplomacy, and governmental institutions.

Does he speak loudly? Absolutely. His sound bites for the media and citizen consumption are so repetitive that audiences can sing along in unison with his words and without the aid of a bouncing ball for syncopation.

Does his body language communicate authority? He uses hand

and arm gestures when reading prepared remarks that more often than not demonstrate that he is far out of his comfort zone on the topic at hand. In meetings with his cabinet, leaders of Congress, and the media, he routinely has his arms folded tightly across his chest, a classic sign of defensive body language, and a lack of self-confidence.

He responds to questions in disorganized ways showing that he may not have heard or understood them or that he prefers to repeat his same tired campaign talking points. The routine exception here is when the vice president is grossly complimenting him and in the process creating his own image concerns in the eyes of the public.

Does the president offer any reason for others to respect him beyond the fact that he has pulled off a P. T. Barnum sucker moment at America's expense? No. The country witnesses his daily histrionics that create far more concern than reassurance. There is little evidence of an upside outcome in store for the country; suspicions of his past behavior on many fronts raise more fear about what's coming next.

His record as president demonstrates he has not personally provided sound input to policy or legislation. Even the tax bill shoved down the throats of Americans was more a matter of wheeling and dealing in Congress to arrive at adequate votes for its passage, and it primarily and overwhelmingly benefited corporate America and the rich. More and more questions are coming up about the true importance of the tax bill and its potential to create new longer term problems. The rich are getting richer—that much is true. He bases his promises and exaggerations on a smoke-and-mirrors approach; his photo-op executive order signings produce little more than that. He must believe his signature makes those orders reality when in fact his signature does little to further any universal and immediate implementation.

The president imagines he is free from fault or defect in his abilities in spite of evidence to the contrary. We are supposed to believe he knows more, can individually do more, develop more, and achieve greater accomplishments than any president in history simply because he says so, and he believes what he says.

He has done little to command the respect of the global community. He offends with actions and words. He shoves a leader to the side to be front and center in a photo. He destroys relationships. He penalizes important allies. He criticizes all. He has seriously damaged the respect the country has historically worked diligently to deserve, and apparently, he has no understanding that aid to other countries is very important to diplomatic relations, options, and success in the short and long terms.

He apparently does not understand the potential his pronouncements have for creating crises and conflict with a variety of audiences. He loves to hear himself repeat his limited vocabulary, and he must believe his tweets are great examples of communication and contributions to great literature. Those who write remarks and speeches for him attempt very hard to portray Trump as intelligent and a leader, but his delivery negates all their work.

Prior to his election, much had been written about Trump's business success, yet many questioned what part of that success Trump was actually responsible for. During the campaign, he spoke about how his business success would make him a better president than anyone in history. To date, that certainly has not occurred because he continues to stagger his way through the responsibilities of the office. He demonstrates freely and exaggeratedly that he is not a manager, and his threats accomplish little. There is no reason to suspect he has any possibility of realizing his boasts about his superiority as president, "more than any in history."

If being incoherent in speech and actions was a prerequisite for his office, Trump has demonstrated his qualifications. Unfortunately as president, he has a daily forum and world stage to routinely articulate his shortcomings without restraint. Predominantly through tweets, sound bites, and impromptu interactions with the media, he attacks those whose experience and knowledge of governing, the Constitution, and diplomacy far exceed his, and he delivers his impressions of what's really important to him. Every interview contains routine praise from himself about himself and criticism of all those who are watching his governing skills and political navigation.

Napoleon said, "Never ascribe to malice that which is adequately explained by incompetence," and he had a point. Trump rarely answers important questions with thoughtful and clear responses. If he feels he is being criticized, he lashes out about how great he is, insults his opponents, demeans his predecessor, and relives the campaign and election as deflections rather than providing direct, meaningful responses. When pressured, he throws out one of his patented, inarticulate, disjointed, and off-point verbal distractions. Perhaps the country should feel sorry for his maladroitness as he drags some Americans into believing his false claims and embarrasses himself and the country at home and abroad. His greatest evolution to date as president is exhibiting his ability to put his childish, narcissistic ways on display.

He was hasty in expounding his lack of knowledge concerning the Affordable Care Act (ACA). He preferred to criticize Obamacare, and at one point, he did not realize that the ACA and what became known as Obamacare were the same. Over time, he has shown that his details deficiency has had a course correction. He criticized his party's leaders and Congress in general but offered nothing more than his usual "repeal and replace" rage.

Congressional requests for him to identify exactly what he was looking for as a health care alternative never came, and even his party's leaders became frustrated with the lack of informed guidance from the president. He never clearly told the public exactly what he was looking for beyond returning to his campaign talking point of "I'm the only one who can fix it." The objective of providing health care improvement is valid, but being only critical of what existed is nonproductive. The country is still waiting.

From the beginning and with abundant frequency since then, Trump has shown that his knowledge on most issues of importance is infinitely shallow. Members of his party became irritated if not shocked as evidence mounted that he was incapable of offering informed guidance. Republicans made their frustration known publicly, but Trump only repeated his campaign boasts, blame-gaming insults, and name-calling. When cornered for a substantive response, he uses this approach as a nonresponse. Members of his party, his cabinet, the Democrats, the Department of Justice, world leaders, adversaries, and others are all targets of his tantrums and pontifications.

Reports have it that the Trump White House playground is marked by a constant shattering of institutions of the democracy, staff and family infighting, and continual exaggeration. Trump has ridden the coattails of success initiated by some of President Obama's programs and even some of Bush's. Trump takes credit for all things that possess a hint of positivity as if to fulfill some inner need to demonstrate these are his own accomplishments, but fact-checks of his boasts disclose his lack of skill and accomplishments. He reportedly does not even work well with others in the White House but does allegedly play well on the golf course.

After nearly two years in office, Trump has demonstrated little ability to make "great deals, the best deals in the history of the country"; he has shown that the word *deal* is simply a word. Even the ghostwriter of *The Art of the Deal*, Tony Schwartz, was quite amazed and frustrated with Trump as he worked on the book and through firsthand observation of deal making. A July 2016 *New Yorker* interview read, "He lied strategically. He had a complete lack of conscience about it." Since most people are "constrained by the truth," Trump's indifference to it "gave him a strange advantage."[130] Consider this questionable attribute while he interacts with North Korea's Kim Jong-un or Russia's Putin. In this interview, Schwartz offered other insights into Trump that perhaps every voter should have read prior to the 2016 election.

Trump floats around like a butterfly looking for a home away from the media, and he uses boasts, lies, and sarcasm as his bee stings.[131] He does not understand that his comments and actions don't demonstrate any expertise, and without fail, the media and others seize the opportunities to inform the public and question his misplaced position as president. Head-in-the-sand support of Trump is dangerous for the country.

Some years back, Lawrence J. Peter postulated a management theory, the Peter Principle, that individuals in a structured organization will be promoted only to their levels of incompetence.[132] Trump may have reached this milestone long before he became president.

CHAPTER 8

THE WATCHDOG MEDIA

The liberty of the press is essential to the security of the state.

—John Adams

The only security of all is in a free press.

—Thomas Jefferson

Adams and Jefferson contributed to the formation of our democracy and its governance by the rule of law. They had witnessed the tyranny of Great Britain's constitutional monarchy, and they recognized the importance of a free press. It is no different today in spite of those who would rather see the press be anything but free.

The press in their times was a point of focus and reference for the colonists and England even before the promulgation of the First Amendment, which reads,[133]

Congress shall make no law respecting an establishment of religion, or prohibiting the free exercise thereof; or abridging the freedom of speech, or of the press; or the right of the people peaceably to assemble, and to petition the Government for a redress of grievances.

Publications took many forms, including pamphlets written by numerous authors such as Thomas Paine and his famous *Common Sense* pamphlet. They provided the colonists an argument for challenging the authority of the British monarchy. Other authors put forth additional propositions for discussion, and still others had the simple goal of informing and inspiring a unity of purpose. In other words, strive to be informed and think about consequences.

However, with the ratification of the Constitution and the establishment of the First Amendment, the press gained momentum and addressed relevant matters without fear of running afoul of the judicial branch.

The media today has continued its governmental watchdog role with great vigor. Each day brings more accusations from the president that the media are determined to destroy him when many see the president doing everything possible to undermine himself and any respect he might deserve.

Technological advancements have enhanced the ability and opportunities for reporters and the public to investigate stories relevant and important to society. Technology has sped up the dissemination of news and has precipitated debate about restraint, national security, and reporter privilege. The media does and should examine ethics and individual behaviors in the essential search for transparency and truth.

Legacy media—print and broadcast—have been joined by competitive options offered by the internet, cable outlets, and other technologically advanced ways of distributing information. All citizens are their own information gatekeepers; they are not dependent solely on the media, a point Trump doesn't seem to grasp. Technology has spawned freedom of expression and innovation as well as fostered the ability of individuals to seek information, and his fake-news claims are an indictment of all free and fact-based thought.

Some have challenged the freedom of the press, and in some cases, outlets have had to resist restraint. Trump does not understand why the First Amendment is in the Constitution; he believes that press reporting is valid only when it compliments him or supports his singular views. Trump attempts to shut down any questioning and criticism of his behavior on so many levels as he maligns the country's institutions and its systems of checks and balances. He attacks voices that confront his uninformed and questionable motives and demand accuracy.

Many have studied prior restraint of the press in matters involving national security, freedom of speech and the press, censorship, intellectual property, and the right to a fair trial. Most notably, the Nixon White House challenged the publication of the Pentagon Papers[134] by the *New York Times*, the *Washington Post*, and other newspapers. Prior restraint became the focus of a landmark case before the Supreme Court, which upheld that an injunction against the newspapers from further publication of the material would be in violation of the First Amendment.[135]

What Trump doesn't seem to comprehend is that the press is not his personal tool for miscommunicating and spreading falsehoods. In his concurring opinion in the 6–3 ruling on the Pentagon Papers case, Supreme Court Justice Hugo Black wrote,

> Now, for the first time in the 182 years since the founding of the Republic, the Federal courts are

asked to hold that the first amendment does not mean what it says, but rather means that the Government can halt the publication of current news of vital importance to the people of this country.

In the First Amendment the Founding Fathers gave the free press the protection it must have to fulfill its essential role in our democracy. The press was to serve the governed, not the governors. The Government's power to censor the press was abolished so that the press would remain forever free to censure the Government. The press was protected so that it could bare the secrets of government and inform the people. Only a free and unrestrained press can effectively expose deception in government.[136]

This is sage advice for all those striving to stifle the media and particularly for Trump, who does not accept the fact that the First Amendment serves all Americans by providing information he may prefer to hide. His camouflaged rhetoric does just the opposite by billboarding his questionable ethics and the missing transparency Americans expect, and that results in disappointments voiced about a flawed president by the global community.

More than forty years after the Pentagon Papers case, technological developments in communications have provided broad access to facts that have befriended the masses and threatened those trying to hide information, deceptive practices, and actions. As important as the internet and other technological tools have become, they frequently foster abuse on the public when mistreated by some whose intentions are more about lies and destruction or simply serve as a soapbox for unsound reasoning.

Trump will continue to be challenged for his lack of reason and facts, but that does not mean the media are making up fake stories. The reporting of Trump's own words is not fake news, though that provokes his threats, rants, claims of false facts, and tweets. The media responsibly point out his inconsistencies, but Trump calls that fake news. Because the president doesn't like to have them pointed out, he will frequently and comically retort, "I didn't say that—it's fake news, fake news." With each repetition of these words, he creates more news he then embellishes ad infinitum rather than accept his shortcomings.

A theme that began in the silly season of Republican primaries was Trump's characterizing anyone who disagreeing with him as incompetent, weak, a loser, and stupid. He bellowed his claim that the media was dishonest just because his comments were not universally accepted. His remarks were challenged and fact-checked, and that bruised his self-image. He lacks the ability to accept accountability for his statements, and his retorts just throw more wood on the fire. His repetitive recourse continues to be to attack, suggest that his often despicable assertions are fact, and thus create even more opportunity for fact-checking that exposes the truth. He is his own worst enemy, and the White House staff has reportedly described him as frequently cruel in his approach that is laced with expletives and circuitous logic. Trump begins his arguments with what he wants to end with ignoring that his premise and his conclusion must be based on facts, truth. It is as if he thinks, *I can't be wrong, so why do I need proof?*

"If the press would cover me accurately and honorably, I would have far less reason to 'tweet.'"[137] Really? The media did not create his personality or reputation. His definition of accuracy is generally suspect, and the chances of his putting a lid on his tweets is likely a bet Las Vegas would not accept.

Walter Lippman, one of the twentieth century's earliest commentators on public opinion, wrote,

> For they are derived, not necessarily by reason, to be sure, but somehow, from the stream of news that reaches the public, and the protection of that stream is the critical interest in a modern state. In going behind opinion to the information which it exploits, and in making the validity of the news our ideal, we shall be fighting the battle where it is really being fought.[138]

If Trump and his people had listened to Lippmann, they might understand that public opinion is not to be controlled but instead to be nurtured with credibility and truth. Trump and his staff can control their messages, but they cannot control the media's scrutiny of those messages. In Trump's case, unfortunately, there is no control at all, and his insincere reading of words off a teleprompter loses credibility when those statements are questioned for clarity and found lacking in that respect. Trumpspeak clutters his messages, and the public focuses on the clutter rather than the meaning and its potential effects.

When Lippmann published his book in 1920, the media landscape was much different. Today, it is not represented only by newspapers and radio broadcasts. Reporters who faced a.m. or p.m. deadlines have gone the way of the five-cent cup of coffee. News now is a 24-7 matter in many forms of media, and the public's access to information has grown to unimaginable levels. People can rapidly get the news and comment on it in many ways and thus potentially influence others in a variety of ways.

Trump undoubtedly worries that the public decides where the truth lies and who it can believe. Thus, a majority of the public is disappointed that the Trump administration is not particularly concerned with the truth, only its manipulated version of it.

Concern about Trump's attempted abuse of power increases, but apparently, Trump is not at all troubled that Americans and leaders around the globe can see through the fog created by tribalism in Washington, Trumpspeak, and a lack of Paine's common sense.

> Good journalism requires more than good journalists. Without an engaged and concerned public, even the most public-minded press cannot do its job. This is precisely the predicament of the press today. It addresses a "public" it does little to help create ... Rather than assuming that a vibrant civic culture exists–or simply lamenting its absence—the public journalist takes responsibility for helping to support and even create it.[139]

The convergence of information provided by the administration and the media's interpreting, questioning, and reporting it have precipitated even greater public doubt and distrust of the Trump administration. At the same time, the drums are beating the need for truth and ethics and even the most basic value—respect.

Are the media misleading the public? Objectivity is always its goal, but when Trump and his favorite media outlet make up their interpretation of reality, objectivity suffers. The media in general become suspect because Trump takes the position that every other news report is fake because these reports do not come from his approved source. People will believe what they want to believe and generally what supports their viewpoints. The credibility of the sources of information, however, presents entirely different issues.

In his somewhat controversial book *What Happened: Inside*

the Bush White House and Washington's Culture of Deception, Scott McClellan, press secretary for President George W. Bush, suggested the political landscape in Washington had become a "permanent campaign." He characterized the game as endless politicking based on the manipulation of shades of truth, partial truths, twisting of truth, and spin. This is quite a commentary on our system of government. Trump and his staff have epitomized McClellan's conclusions.

> The permanent campaign also ensnares the media who become complicit enablers of its polarizing effects. They emphasize conflict, controversy, and negativity, focusing not on the real-world impact of policies and their larger underlying truths but on the horse races aspect of politics—who's winning, who's losing and why.[140]

What McClellan did not state is that responsible watchdog journalism commands a dedication to facts and truth.

Consider today's president and what he provides each day—conflict, controversy, and negativity. It is not with a great degree of anticipation that the media does not have to look for these things because the president's greatest skill may well be egotistically creating them. As a reminder, Trump began his reelection campaign after being in office for less than a month, and his platform endlessly relived the 2016 campaign. Instead of staging rallies and fundraising activities, he should have learned what being president requires, but unfortunately, he has apparently not embarked on that process. Hindsight in this case helps us consider what might have been if Trump understood his responsibilities and operated in respectful ways.

At one point in his life, Trump thought he understood the

media, which he embraced because they worked for him in his real estate development world.

> One thing I've learned about the press is that they're always hungry for a good story, and the more sensational the better. It's in the nature of the job, and I understand that. The point is that if you are a little different, or a little outrageous, or if you do things that are bold or controversial, the press is going to write about you.[103]

Without question, Trump is outrageous, bold, controversial, and much more, and the media does give him column inches and air time, but now, he is not enjoying the coverage.

His incessant tweets betray him as he criticizes those who call him out—and no, not just the media—and he is the ultimate example of someone not responding well to any suggestion his statements are incorrect. Smartphones do not require those who tweet to be overly correct, so we can understand why Trump uses that medium, but whether his words are spoken or tweeted, there is a consistency there. He impulsively reacts and shares whatever enters his mind, and he travels far afield and makes politically incorrect statements on most any subject. He offends and embarrasses the country, and he displays minimal knowledge on the topic of the moment. He seems to think the media and the country should just accept and not rebut or challenge his thinking. Something for him to consider—it is not just the media that are watching, listening, and reading.

It was not a Sun Tzu–inspired strategy[71] Trump employed when he came up with the concept of fake news; it is his excuse for his every mistake, miscue, offensive protocol misfire, and exhibition of cluelessness. His relentless attacks on the media imply that every story he does not like or every question about his latest irrational response is fake news. Fake news has become the umbrella Trump opens to shield himself from his shortcomings, but the term provides little cover as the sun illuminates the truth. That's the real news.

One widely discussed rumor during the primaries was that Trump was just stroking his ego and was preparing to start another venture in the form of a news network. If that ever became reality, fake news would likely take on an entirely new meaning devoid of facts, truth, ethics, and informed insight.

His shouts of fake news has reached ridiculous and irrelevant heights; it has become a derogatory defense for everything that doesn't go his way or that doesn't parrot his opinions and words. The term has invaded the dialogue of politicians and his base of supporters to the point that it is the go-to defense tactic with each new outrageous comment from Trump. The concerns of Americans who doubt his competency and effectiveness as president are not fake; Trump makes their concerns extraordinarily real.

The press has historically and rightfully taken the view that the First Amendment is to keep the public informed. In its consistent watchdog role, the press has pursued information through official and unofficial sources. Technology has made documenting proof sources easier as well. The Freedom of Information Act has provided access to documents and the truth. The difference between the media and Trump is that the former engage in fact-checking while the latter does not.

The United Nations recognized the importance of free expression in 1948.

> Everyone has the right to freedom of opinion and expression; this right includes freedom to hold opinions without interference, and to seek, receive,

and impart information and ideas through any
media, regardless of frontiers.[141]

More recently, the UN recognized that press freedom is essential
for good governance as it "can ensure transparency, accountability,
and the rule of law."[142] It may be too much of a leap to think
Trump embraces transparency, accountability, and the rule of
law. Trump's indictment of the media through constant criticism
becomes a distraction that allows him to skirt his hopelessness as
president. The news is indeed all about him, a frequent product
of his narcissism, and that is unlikely to change. Trump's creation
of the toxic personal idiom of fake news must be a source of pride
for him. He refers to a news organization as fake news. He refers
to reporting on his words as fake news. He refers to individuals
as fake news, and easily tosses the term around whenever he is
unable to come up with an intelligent response to reasonable
questions from any source. He fogs over the fact that questions can
legitimately challenge his unsubstantiated statements.

Consider this: the pope felt compelled to comment on the
meaning of fake news as the phrase became more widespread
around the world thanks to Trump. The pope's conclusion was
revealing and perhaps educational for Trump. The pope defined
fake news as the spreading of disinformation online or in traditional
media.

> Disinformation thus thrives on the absence of healthy
> confrontation with other sources of information
> that could effectively challenge prejudices and
> generate constructive dialogue; instead, it risks
> turning people into unwilling accomplices in
> spreading biased and baseless ideas.[143]

This is appropriate food for thought for the president before he embarks on his disinformation claims. Dialogue is critical, but with Trump, there is no dialogue—only banter by and about himself and directed to his supporters, who absorb his every word as truth. Trump thinks the only good ideas are those he professes, but they most often fall short of being good or even logical.

The freedom to disagree with others is essential for our democracy to function the way the founding fathers intended it, not what Trump perceives it to be. Any disagreement with his political repartee precipitates his criticism of those doing the disagreeing, including other countries. He routinely makes a mockery of any hope of intellectual debate.

Members of Congress and some in his party are not comfortable with his criticism of the media. Senator John McCain wrote,

> Without strong leadership in the White House, Congress must commit to protecting independent journalism, preserving an open and free media environment, and defending the fundamental right to freedom of opinion and expression.[144]

With all that he faced with his health and his future, Senator McCain represented the type of leader who didn't seek universal support of his views but nevertheless gained wide respect domestically and internationally.

The media's difficult challenge is keeping up with and commenting on Trump's daily missteps, misrepresentations, contradictions, walk-backs, questionable interactions, notable and suspected conflict-of-interest concerns, biases, and ineptitude, including that of his advisers and staff members. Shouting fake news just doesn't compute. Trump overlooks the fact that his need to be in the spotlight does not give him control, nor should it. Coverage of his shortcomings creates the news he calls fake. To paraphrase a noted philosopher of our times, Forrest Gump, "Fake is as fake does."[145] As president, Trump routinely embarrasses the United States and is conceivably leading the country into a constitutional crisis that becomes more of a possibility each day.

Just observing Trump in the presence of reputable world figures is illuminating. During the NATO leaders' conference in May 2017, a camera caught Trump very clearly pushing the prime minister of Montenegro aside to be in front of a group, and he sported his tough-guy "I'm the greatest" expression. At the G20 conference in July 2017, video coverage demonstrated that rarely was the president sought out in social settings as he wandered aimlessly around the room clearly out of his element.

The media, and not just the US media, legitimately report his comments and tweets emanating from such gatherings, but he focuses his negativism on the US pool of reporters on-site and at home. Perhaps he is leery of his base starting to understand what their votes have created; his checking a box or two next to his campaign promises that show no substantive benefits for them will reach the point of disappointing those supporters as well.

Trump shocked the world by pulling US support from the Paris Climate Accord. He has stated on numerous occasions that climate change is a hoax. As a leading advocate for raising awareness and action on climate change, former vice president Al Gore has become convinced that Trump also has many climate deniers in his White House.[146] The reasons Trump gave for his withdrawal from the Paris Accord were flawed, and leaders from around the world as well as US business leaders were stunned at his action. Should the media have just ignored the detrimental significance of his move and the resulting lack of US cooperation in saving the planet? Hardly fake news.

Watching the president read a speech from a teleprompter,

including the Paris Accord withdrawal announcement, is striking. First, it is clear that he doesn't necessarily understand what he is saying; he uses words that he does not use in normal conversation, and he frequently mispronounces them. Second, Trump cannot stay on script. He apparently feels he must ad-lib for emphasis, which in most cases are repetitions of his stale jargon that make him look foolish. He brings up the media at every opportunity; he overlooks the possibility that he is making the media his adversary by not displaying knowledge of the facts and details surrounding any topic he speaks on. One of his frequent ad-libs is, "Believe me," but no matter how often he voices those words, the likelihood that anything he says will be believed is continually diminishing even among those who would very much like to believe him. "Believe me" is often followed by, "I have to tell ya." No you don't, Mr. President. We've heard it before.

Trump tries to create the impression of a news media operating like a pack of vigilantes bent on criticizing his every move. As easily as that paranoid view might come to him, such an overarching indictment of the profession of journalism is significantly misplaced. Certain tenets of the profession guide its participants. One such guidance is what has been termed the Principles of Journalism.[147]

1. Journalism's first obligation is to the truth.
2. Its first loyalty is to citizens.
3. Its essence is a discipline of verification.
4. Its practitioners must maintain an independence from those they cover.
5. It must serve as an independent monitor of power.
6. It must provide a forum for public criticism and compromise.
7. It must strive to make the significant interesting and relevant.

8. It must keep the news comprehensive and proportional.
9. Its practitioners must be allowed to exercise their personal conscience.

The first two principles above speak to the journalistic necessity of reporting truthfully as an obligation to all and to do so in such a way that the public recognizes that being informed by the media is a demonstration of its loyalty and discipline. Verification is achieved through fact-checking and the use of multiple sources for credibility and insight.

Journalists do not serve individuals, and that includes the president; journalists and the president serve the people. By serving as governmental watchdogs, journalists provide citizens with information that may affect their lives. Awareness that the media provide sanctions citizens to pursue more knowledge on their own that can contribute to, enhance, or modify their opinions and decisions. The media provide opportunities for citizens to respond and discuss whatever it reports. Interpretative and investigative reporting provides depth, timeliness, and education.

The subject matter dictates specific topics, direction for inquiry, and appropriate balance for understanding. We all have biases resulting from many factors—how we were raised and educated and what experiences we have had. Journalists are no different, but they strive to remain objective in their reporting, and frequently, their conscious and subconscious experiences will spawn new areas of questioning and investigation.

Trump's administration is not a narrow field for the media. He and his staff, advisers, and family create the news in new ways and with repetitive frequency. Where reporters and editors spend considerable time confirming and editing stories, the Trump administration has considerable difficulty in editing itself. In instances when reports feature something positive Trump has said or done, in short order, he becomes his own worst enemy. He will frequently reconsider his actions and turn a story in a decidedly different direction by tweeting a condescending remark about someone or a criticizing the media. He repeatedly skewers his foot with barbed remarks in an attempt to be critical of someone or something else. Because Trump is universally erratic, the media are constantly rewriting, and Trump shoots his fake news arrows in multiple directions. The media cannot follow a path of absolution when it comes to the Trump administration's faux pas and its desire to be represented as doing great things.

Ignoring stories that Trump would rather not be reported does not make them go away. It is not the responsibility of the news media to create a more democratic society but rather to support it. Journalists contribute information that will help the public assess what they believe is right or wrong for them and the country; this information does not come solely from the White House.

There are some media outlets that seem to want to incite controversy at every turn, and they include the outlet the president seems most loyal to him. To the media's credit, sensationalist reporting is not the norm, but it does occur, and when it does, the motives of the source of that reporting must be examined. If an ideological bias—conservative or liberal—is driving reporting, the principles of journalism are not being rigidly followed.

> Were it left to me to decide whether we should have a government without newspapers, or newspapers without a government, I should not hesitate a moment to prefer the latter.

—Thomas Jefferson

What Thomas Jefferson could not have anticipated when he

made this statement is how the country would evolve over decades of technological advancement, controversy, wars, internal strife, corruption, and the like and what role that newspapers and now the media in many forms play in informing the public. You can substitute *media* for *newspapers*, but Jefferson's point remains clear. He believed in an informed electorate without political interference.

Fundamentally, there are three areas that can be rightfully considered in an ethics-based discussion of the freedom of the press—the public's right, need, and desire to know. Some believe that these three areas are to be tempered by an interpretation of the information and its potential negative impact on national security. Most will agree that harm can come out of the releasing and publishing of classified information intentional or not. Trump overlooked this concept when he disclosed intelligence from an Israeli counterterrorism operation to the Russian ambassador and in the same meeting referred to his firing of James Comey as relieving great pressure on him.[148] More recently, questions have been raised about what he and Putin discussed in their private meeting in Helsinki.

Those who are intent on hampering if not blocking professional journalists from executing integrity and judgment in their reporting are doing exactly what the founding fathers wanted to avoid. Today, the constant lying, the impeding access to, and the manipulation of information coming from the White House is the root of the issue, and the resulting reporting demonstrates the administration's lack of interest in what the public has a right, need, and desire to know. Ethics and transparency are absent, and the only apparent matter of importance is the president's desire to ignore the country's relevant interests and needs and instead look only for personal wins. Those routinely applauding his egocentric actions also exhibit a common characteristic of going only as deep as a tweet or a headline to form their opinions. That is all these individuals feel they need to know.

The public desires to know the workings of the government, the abilities of those in power, and other matters of importance. The exceptions to the public's wants and the ability of the press to meet them are subject to the law. The wants are not always universal; they can at times be particular. Different people require different information to make informed decisions.

What does the public need to know? The most obvious response to this question is that the public must be informed. Broad generalizations from the president or members of Congress are insufficient when livelihoods are at stake domestically or abroad and certainly if a military conflict could occur. How many Americans truly understand why we are sending our forces to Syria, Nigeria, and Afghanistan? Why are those stationed at the DMZ in Korea and other hot spots around the world necessary? Sadly, the response most often given by those in authority is "We are protecting our national security." Should Americans simply accept that response and sleep well at night, or do they need more information on which to develop a broader understanding? I hope those in government would say it was the latter, but consistently hiding behind the veil of national security with no explanation results in an under-informed population.

Trump has little understanding himself; he instead prefers to gin up his base of supporters with absurd and occasionally obscene remarks. His flip-flopping on positions is hard to follow or understand, so the public is left needing to know more.

What does the public have a right to know? Truth above all. It was clear that Trump had a difficult time with the truth even before he took office. Perhaps he had no trouble with determining what is true but instead with how much he would twist and manipulate facts into a narrative that pleased him while rarely informing the public. This approach gives more substance to the proposition that Trump is playing at being president.

The public has the right to information that will help it monitor and question its leaders. Citizens will then know their leaders' intentions, and that will allow them to contribute meaningfully to the country. Even with his autocratic—approaching dictatorial—style, Trump cannot choose to keep the public guessing for much longer as once it gains its access to truth this will provide the linchpin for change and accountability.

The Latin phrase *lux et veritas*, light and truth, shall guide the United States. Presidents, members of Congress, and leaders of essential government agencies come and go, but the citizens of the United States are the constant in our democracy. They are the foundation and backbone of progress, but without access to truth, the light of the country will be irreparably dimmed.

> *When the public's right to know is threatened, and when the rights of free speech and free press are at risk, all of the other liberties we hold dear are endangered.*[149]

CHAPTER 9

WAKE UP, AMERICA

Eternal vigilance is an essential element of a democratic system. A citizenry that takes the good judgment of its leaders for granted is a society that leaves itself vulnerable to disappointment and failure.

—Thomas Jefferson

Years ago, Jefferson provided a resounding assessment of where the United States finds itself today as good judgment from Trump is rarely evident. Everything is singularly about him, not the country. Continued subjection to falsehood and manipulation by the president and his administration will lead continually to disappointment and failure.

Can Congress act responsibly and work for the country, not for its members' ideological biases? There are occasional flickers of light and enlightenment that point to cooperation between the political parties, but these fade almost as soon as they occur.

Must we continue to allow the attacks on essential institutions of our democracy, most specifically on the DOJ and those in

Congress seeking truth? The president intervenes in areas that are not his to influence or demand, and Congress has not adequately exercised the checks on the presidency the Constitution provides it. Trump-related questions are being investigated by those he appointed to the DOJ and those appointed by that body's leadership. Trump is not behaving like an innocent individual; the more the truth and suspicions surface, the more he levels attacks to distract. He continues to criticize his attorney general for recusing himself from the campaign investigation over a year and a half ago, but to what end? Trump can fire his AG at any time, but should that occur, the AG would no longer be restrained from answering more-specific questions about the campaign. Fortunately, the DOJ comprises people who are committed to truth, ethics, integrity, and diligence.

It seems that every day, something untoward takes place in the White House, at Mar-a-Lago, or on Air Force One through extemporaneous interactions with the media, at press briefings, or meetings with world leaders. Trump then attempts to absolve himself from controversy that most generally he has created. He posts an outrageous tweet that exposes his bizarre thinking, and he then undermines his press secretary's credibility by forcing a misguided defense—facts be damned.

Partisan infighting in Congress dampens the prospects for real progress on multiple fronts. Another unqualified Trump appointee resigns due to unrestrained oversight or ethics issues, and others are discovered not to have full security clearances and yet are handling classified material in cavalier ways. New discoveries surface about family business interests and favors that could be tied to efforts to influence domestic and international policy. And when speaking, Trump invariably steps on members of Congress, his cabinet, or the media because he can or perhaps because he doesn't have the ability to censor himself. Yet without fail, his supporters at his rallies are delirious with praise. President Jefferson, where is their vigilance? Are they expressing good judgment?

Our country has always been subject to the rule of law, not the rule of a self-centered and uninformed president who seems to feel he is above the law. Verbal smoke screens and fabrications will not safeguard America or allow it to progress domestically and abroad. Perhaps Plato got it right centuries ago: "The price of apathy towards public affairs is to be ruled by evil men."

Narcissism has led Trump to the state of indifference. Saying something only to appease his supporters and their subsequent cheers shows no understanding of leadership or accomplishment. Saying one thing but doing something far different muddies the waters considerably for those whose motives are far more respectable. His speeches are full of errors and false claims. He enables others, like the vice president, who fawn over his every word. His exaggerated ad-libs when speaking in any forum are something else. Is it Trump's objective to show he is all knowing and powerful, or does he just have no control over what he says? It is painful to watch him struggle to put a sentence together without repeating words and then circling back and repeating them again leaving those on the receiving end with little substance. His proclivity to deflect shows maliciousness and at times potentially something far worse. Nevertheless, his supporters at rallies soak it all up as if his words were coming from a burning bush.

Citizens can hold Trump and his party accountable, and it is time for that. Trump chooses to blame the Democrats for his legislative failures, but the true failing is in the seemingly unlikely possibility of the two parties working in concert toward a shared end owing to the lack of true leadership. Dedication to achieving a common goal is laudable, but the president is not leading in any way, and he doesn't seem to have the ability to broker that deal. Worse still, he doesn't seem to care; he relies on his party leaders to make all things happen, including twisting a few Democratic arms for necessary votes, but with little success.

His base got him into the White House, and the rest of Americans resigned themselves to hoping he would succeed as president. No one objectively wanted him to fail because too much was at stake. There were to be at least four years of a Trump administration (barring his fall from grace as he ultimately faces the great Mueller reveal), so whether he was someone's hero or someone else's default president of the moment, those four years needed to account for something.

He had issues to address and problems to solve, and the thinking was that perhaps his windy campaign promises could turn into something positive. What was not known of course was that while Americans may have wanted to believe that he might achieve responsible and ethical outcomes postelection, Trump has consistently shown that he does not have the ability to achieve sustained success by any definition. It quickly became evident that the presidency was more of a game, a pastime for him, and not a commitment to the country. It quickly became all about him.

Every morning, the world awakens and asks, "What's next with Trump?" He answers with worries about disorder, new and repeated false claims, lies, and cover-ups. For all the comfort they may provide him, Trump's statements are most like those of an immature adolescent who has wrecked his parent's car and is trying to hide that fact.

Though it seems an unattainable dream, wouldn't it be wonderful if those elected to serve the country put their egos, ideological rants, and bickering aside? Far too few in Congress on either side of the aisle have stood up to create an environment of sustained cooperation for the common good while holding the president accountable. Backbones have disappeared, and the power struggles in Congress looked toward the midterm elections in

2018. The elections result: one party no longer controls Congress. Trump spends little time being a true president; instead, he watches television in fear of someone criticizing him and then takes every opportunity to showcase the shallowness of his abilities in his Twitter defenses.

Trump's definition of leadership is based on pushing all others aside so he will be at the front of his parade. Those who follow him keep busy stepping around and over what he leaves behind. It is clear from his public statements that he cannot provide clear direction for Congress much less the country. On more than one occasion, his party leaders have complained, "We don't know what he wants." Trump talks in repetitive subheads punctuated by threats. He does not have patience for criticism of any type or for those who suggest alternatives to his positions or actions. Without fail, he will do most anything to distract and deflect attention from the investigation of the special prosecutor with the exception of his repeated "No collusion!" denial.

What is undoubtedly most frustrating for him are charges levied, plea deals reached, acknowledgments of guilt, and jail sentences for others. What has surfaced to this point may be just the beginning for the special counsel. As Trump continues to act out in childish ways, he shows his nervous and perhaps guilty cards in his daily presidential poker game. He attempts to try his case before the court of public opinion without recognizing that the majority of Americans remain suspicious of him. He has polarized the country to the point that even when they hear the truth presented, he and his supporters deny it. When he demonizes immigrants, his party embraces his words. There are so many Trump targets to address. The special prosecutor isn't silent because he has nothing to say. As a true and ethical professional, he will ultimately be heard.

The strongest democracies flourish from frequent and lively debate, but they endure when people of every background and belief find a way to set aside smaller differences in service of a greater purpose.[150]

—President Barack Obama

Trump does not confer with anyone beyond those he thinks will compliment him in some fashion. He leaves true discourse to others. At least, he should receive credit for that as he recognizes that patience, study, and intelligent discussion are not his strong suit. He tries to intimidate by presenting disjointed topics. Trump has repeatedly shown that he does not respect people with experience, even those he has appointed to his administration.

It is impossible for Trump to set aside small differences. He routinely tells Americans and the world that he knows all and that his opinion is all that counts. Those who do not fit Trump's definition of loyal are subjected to his tweets and misrepresentations. Trump overlooks the fact that those in government and particularly those in the DOJ owe their loyalty to the Constitution and the people of this country. President Nixon's infamous enemies list,[151] which started with twenty names, expanded to include a much larger number of people across all demographics. Evidence to date shows that members of the media head Trump's enemies list. He has stated that the "media is the enemy of the people," an insult of massive proportions to the founding fathers, the Constitution, the First Amendment, and responsible journalists who work diligently to reveal truth, not report an individual's version of it.

However, the media are not alone on that list; he has targeted members of both parties, celebrities, and even a cadre of former members of the CIA, FBI, and DOJ who have spoken out in opposition to and with informed concern about his policies and actions and his lack of knowledge and understanding. He also apparently doesn't understand that for any president, loyalty among other positive attributes is defined by carrying out the oath of office, not by being loyal to an individual. It's worth repeating.

> I do solemnly swear (or affirm) that I will faithfully execute the office of president of the United States, and will to the best of my ability, preserve, protect and defend the Constitution of the United States.[152]

The oath sets out very clearly what may be Trump's Achilles' heel—"to the best of my ability." How much longer can the country tolerate example after example that creating disorder, demonstrating ineptitude, and making inflammatory statements are his most visible abilities? What is Trump's purpose? To win of course even if it is at the expense of the country and its citizens.

So far, his winning objective has shown little in the way of benefits for all citizens. His family and his wealthy and big business supporters have won with the tax plan passed by Congress, but as the curtain has been pulled back with analysis after analysis by well-informed and intelligent people, Trump is in no way preserving, protecting, and defending the Constitution. He is defending himself with all the legal wrangling he can muster but not with a focus on the Constitution and people.

A nation of sheep will beget a government of wolves.[153]

America, it is time to wake up. The country is being pulled apart by a president who has no inkling how to unify, work cooperatively, and run a massive organization—the government—that is far more difficult to run than any dealings of his past. Wining is not the objective. Negotiation is not built on overpowering others with trickery, humiliating those on the other side of an issue, or even taking advantage of someone else's failings to somehow show that this would enhance Trump's stature and image. As Ted Kennedy stated, "Integrity is the lifeblood of democracy. Deceit is a poison in its veins."[154]

Trump made one revealing statement long before he entered politics and ran for office: "You can't con people, at least not for long. You can create excitement, you can do wonderful promotion and get all kinds of press, and you can throw in a little hyperbole. But if you don't deliver the goods, people will eventually catch on."[104]

People are indeed catching on, but that intelligent movement by the masses needs a strong dose of informed awareness, enthusiasm, and action. Trump has become so partisan in his orientation and dealings with others that he does not distinguish between the Democratic Party's defense of its ideology and objectives and democracy itself. He apparently would be hard pressed to recite the historic principles of the Republican Party because he embraces little that doesn't emanate from the touchpad on his smartphone and the extremes of his inner circle's thinking. Trump is not a wizard in any form. He acts unreasonably and is not truly putting Americans first or making the country great.

The power of our government is vested in its citizens, and politicians are to treat their constituents with honesty, integrity, and transparency. When this charge is weakened, ignored, or tarnished, political disorder can result and government order and authority can become compromised. Anarchy? Perhaps, but it is time to make the president accountable for his actions and words and not make excuses for him; he has lost and should play his game no more. Is there anything about his profile that makes everyone sleep better at night because he is our commander in chief? Trump's Twitter subjects are far reaching, but the outcome of his diatribes are the same. There is little provided in his misinformation campaign that is of value to the country and instead contributes only to his egocentric reign of terror and division.

The late jazz singer and composer Mose Allison penned the lyrics to the song "Your Mind Is on Vacation"[155] that appropriately describe the litany of vitriol and inaccurate statements that frequently bear witness to Trump's lack of suitability for the office.

> *You're sitting there yakkin' right in my face*
> *I guess I'm gonna have to put you in your place*
> *Y'know if silence was golden, you couldn't raise a dime*
> *Because your mind is on vacation and your mouth is working overtime*

Rest in peace, Mose.

What is most disturbing for many are Trump's never-ending attacks on the DOJ and in particular the FBI. These personal attacks (e.g., on James Comey, Jeff Sessions, Rob Rosenstein, Robert Mueller, Sally Yates, and others) illustrate that Trump believes that the DOJ and its agencies work for him and that its staff should act in whatever way he dictates. This is yet another example of how little Trump knows about the branches of the government, their boundaries of authority, and their relationships to the function of our democratic system.

Tyrants are rarely open to exposures of reality. Though DOJ employees demonstrate that they will not let the president bully them and that their history of service to the country is well documented, Trump will attempt to tear them down. When he thinks he is under scrutiny by many and not just by the DOJ and more specifically by the FBI and a special prosecutor, his rhetoric becomes more convoluted. He berated Comey to say he was not being investigated as if that would wipe truth from the files and he could live on in his world of falsity. The American population may never know the total number of questionable acts he has perpetrated, but as the dots are connected, it will be quite remarkable to witness Trump's next steps.

> *Public corruption is the FBI's top criminal priority. The threat—which involves the corruption of local, state, and federally elected, appointed, or contracted officials—strikes at the heart of government, eroding public confidence and undermining the strength of our democracy.*[156]

James Comey said that years before Trump became president; it points out why this country should wake up. The Trump presidency and administration cannot continue on a path of inappropriate, bizarre, and narcissistic destruction with little interest in the impact of its actions or lack thereof on the country and the world.

Immigrants, who are being discriminated against, have a far more constructive vision for our country, their opportunities, and their responsibilities than Trump is willing to understand. Could Trump pass the citizenship test? With notable exceptions, members of Congress are at odds with each other, the president, and anyone who speaks out about the chaos Trump has created with his racist approach to immigration.

It is time to stand up. Under Trump, the country is thrashing about, and the prospects for it not moving forward in meaningful ways are frightening. His continual attacks on institutions, regulations, and people suggest there is no order in the administration or the man. Statements are made and tweets are posted; the White House staff then defends them and tries to make sense of them and in the process contributes to the deflections that seem to be Trump's standard operating procedure. How do they sleep at night? The public struggles to understand Trump and his misspeaks, and as a result, some may be taking their eyes off the bedlam.

We should put our hopes in the integrity of the DOJ despite Trump's attempts to undermine it. Obstruction of justice is not just a phrase to be bantered about by those in Congress or denied by Trump as he boasts repeatedly about what others are investigating. It is a real and important component of our rule of law. If investigations reveal links between Trump and Russia, his campaign and his administration will represent the election of a severely flawed and unethical individual and further shred the United States' global reputation. If and when the opportunity presents itself—and many believe that will eventually occur—the legislative and judicial branches of government can rescue the country and its citizens through the due process Trump speaks about but clearly does not comprehend. Truth will prevail, not manipulation and ignorance.

Some have compared Trump's dysfunction to Nixon's paranoid reign; these comparisons speak to their shared desire for absolute power. In an interview with *The Telegraph* in the UK, John Dean, former White House counsel in the Nixon administration, provided an insightful and chilling perception: "They're very different in their perception of the president's authority," Dean said according to the newspaper. "Trump is more dangerous because he doesn't know what he's doing. The danger is he could do anything."[157]

It's difficult to argue with Dean's assessment. The impulsive gene that seems to guide Trump is troubling to witness, and in the short and long terms, it's potentially dangerous. He disregards the potential consequences of his actions in his desire for omnipotence. He forgets or disregards the impact on people even when he feeds his base his nursery rhyme of the day. A reasonable example is his tariffs on foreign products and the impact these imprudent moves could have on the workforce here, increased costs for manufacturers and thus consumers, fewer exports, and so on. He is simply flexing his muscles in front of a mirror. Dean and Justice Black are correct; Trump is not serving the governed, only himself.

"Make America Great Again" and "America First" were his campaign slogans, but history records these are not original in politics. The Republican Party has routinely injected President Reagan into political discourse, and in his 1980 presidential campaign, his slogan was "Let's Make America Great Again." Coincidence? Most likely not as his campaign creators may have wanted to associate Trump with Reagan.

Another moment in presidential history relates to the Trump campaign's efforts to position him. In 1920, Warren G. Harding used "America First" as his slogan, but that's not where the similarity ends. At the time, this slogan was associated with strong isolationist and anti-immigrant feelings following World War I. After his death, his presidency was disgraced because of scandals relating to members of his cabinet and the reveal of his extramarital affairs. History has ranked his presidency as one of the worst.

Trump brought his flashy brand to the White House but little in the way of qualifications. He has also brought another component—his own form of terrorism. In his case, it doesn't involve missiles, guns, bombs, or even cyberattacks on individuals or institutions. He engages in psychological terrorism; his verbal assaults and false claims are meant to defend his political and personal agendas; he has decided that what he says must be correct. His rapid-fire tweets do little to enhance whatever credibility he has left.

His tactics of intimidation inflame racism and disparage women. False statements are the staple of his communication style, and his nepotism creates credibility rifts in his administration. He divides Congress and harms important global relationships. All these shortcomings contribute to his chaotic administration's ongoing lack of effectiveness.

His personal terrorism has the world's attention; leaders in other countries are fearful of his childish threats to retaliate economically against them. But the fear that keeps people up at night is Trump's famous name-calling of Kim Jong-un and threatening to devastate North Korea while Kim continued to build up his country's nuclear capabilities. Trump's terrorism using Twitter is preposterous.

> North Korean Leader Kim Jong Un just stated that the "Nuclear Button is on his desk at all times." Will someone from his depleted and food starved regime please inform him that I too have a Nuclear Button, but it is a much bigger & more powerful one than his, and my Button works![158]

If this tweet wasn't so ill advised, it would be laughable. To be fair, Kim played this ping-pong game of insulting as well. Trump's handling of the on-and-off summit with Kim was a miniseries of Trump's reality-show presidency. Many were concerned that Trump would not be prepared to negotiate or be in a position to deal with Kim's history and North Korea's previous walks of power and its promises broken. Perhaps Trump didn't realize that even photos of the two of them together was a propaganda win for Kim, not a chest-thumping moment for the US leader.

In advance of the summit, Trump worked on a self-fulfilling prophecy of failure by threatening to "walk away" if the discussions were not fruitful even before the details of the meeting were established. Seasoned diplomats feared Trump would walk into the meeting with an unrealistic, first-strike goal of total denuclearization that history has demonstrated would not have been a realistic expectation. The potential for first-step diplomacy was not on his radar; it was all or nothing. As a nonstudent of history, he flounders in settings that do not allow him to win on all levels particularly when his opponent has a strategic intellect. The result of the summit: a brief signed document that represents nothing new of significance from prior negotiations with the historic Kim dynasty.

The majority of Americans have long passed the milestone of being patient with Trump. The petulant child does not project success; he should fear that a time-out is coming. People of reason and law are closer than they may appear in his personal rearview mirror. And those who are lawless, including his apparent friend Putin and other dictators around the world he has complimented, will not repay Trump's kindness but will get his attention in other ways that will be troubling if not terroristic for America.

It appears that because Trump is averse to researching most any subject before he speaks, he demonstrates that he understands little about the topic or the impact of his uninformed banter. In important meetings with global supporters or those he is courting such as Kim and Putin, it appears he is unprepared as even reading from notes is a struggle for him. He counts on his personality to win over the most resistant opponent. He grossly exaggerates positive outcomes of his interactions, and in some cases—most notably his private meeting with Putin—the concessions, promises, and agreements he may have made are clouded in mystery. He is keeping even the country's intelligence agencies in the dark as he boasts about the summit's success. Study the expressions and body language of the two players in the video coverage of their initial handshakes and at the press conference after their meeting. Putin looks as though he has just received the keys to the vault as Trump seemingly prostrates himself in front of his friend.

Trump is out of touch with the wants and needs of the country, and he does not know how to develop an agenda to get things done. If he is leaving the research and evaluation to those around him, there is little evidence that they have had an impact on him or that they have gotten him to listen to facts. Of course, he could just be summarily ignoring them because he knows more than anyone else. Right. Considering the players, perhaps it is all these possibilities as their personal agendas are not well hidden. Are the insiders trying desperately to just hang on as they negotiate their individual book deals with publishers? Perhaps, but the rest of the country is not such an insider, so it is rightfully concerned about where the country is headed and how it might be hurt.

By constantly focusing on himself, taking offense at the most inconsequential things, and criticizing and misrepresenting media reporting, he fosters disarray in the country. He has divided it in innumerable ways, and he seems oblivious to the fact that he is ridiculed and not respected around the world. The great manipulator doesn't recognize he is being manipulated, and the best example of this may be his allegiance to Putin. Now that is *sad*—to use one of his most frequently used tweet words. He says he loves America, but that is patently not to his detriment and it is suspiciously only when it benefits him.

There are no secrets time does not ultimately reveal,[159] but can the country afford to wait for that time while Trump continues his amateur games? Trump is quick to say, "We'll have to wait and see" to most any inquiry that requires critical thinking, yet it has been repeatedly shown that waiting brings only more rash actions and outlandish statements. Trump incessantly talks about making a deal, but that word has the sound of something far from ethical and aboveboard; it rings of divisive manipulation, falsehood, and questionable ethics as he tries so very hard to show his power and control. In his world, a deal is only about him personally winning on some level.

How much longer do Americans and the world have to spend being pummeled with commentary about Trump's personal failings and the allegations made about him? Examples of his ineffectual attempt at governing punctuated by threats of one type or another go out to a cacophony of audiences. Think about the time wasted as the country waits. This is not an example of presidential behavior or competency. He talks and talks but offers the country little assurance. "Acting" presidential is not part of the president's job description.

After six months in office, Trump spoke this insult about one who had previously led the country. "With the exception of the late, great Abraham Lincoln, I can be more presidential than any president that's ever held this office."[160] The content of Trump's statement aside, this inappropriate reference to President Lincoln, who is universally respected as a great leader, is disturbingly unfortunate.

President Lincoln once made the following statement about a political opponent: "He can compress the most words into the smallest idea of any man I have ever met." Lincoln might describe Trump as using repetitive words with the smallest amount of logic and meaning in the loudest voice that accomplishes little. Would Lincoln support Trump as the leader of today's Republicans? Lincoln would be embarrassed to do so.

The Trump approach to the presidency mirrors his approach to his life. It is always and forever all about him. The presidency is not intended to just be the next reincarnation of his reality game show. Unfortunately the reality he has created thus far is not entertainment. It is a tragic assault on respectable values, institutions, the Constitution, and people. Trump's focus on personal wins at all costs has placed real progress, solutions, and democracy so far in the background that Americans are facing a steep and troublesome climb from the depths of the disorder he is creating. Trump thrives on controversy and the more he sees his image and comments reflected in media of all forms he will say and do most anything to further precipitate that coverage. The media that he is quick to criticize, while journalists pursue and defend the First Amendment, feed his narcissistic needs. Unfortunately at the same time the media is being played by the outrageous con promulgated by the president. Ignoring Trump's behavior is not an option.

Chairman Mao Zedong, the historic leader of the Communist Party in China, provided some solace for America in his statement "It's always darkest before the dawn." Each day, Trump contributes to what appears to be infinite darkness. As dawn approaches, it is possible that it will become even clearer that he is dragging the country down so far that rising from the chaos will require a unity of purpose from Americans that supersedes any ideological orientation.

To be continued? Please, no.

Wake up, America.

EPILOGUE

I began writing this book to evaluate what I felt was an incredibly ruthless and disturbing chapter in US history. I have been a student of history and in particular US history since my elementary school years; that continued through college, where the subject was my second major. History makes up the vast majority of books I read, and my personal library includes a deep repository of books about our founding fathers and presidents.

My library provides documentation of seminal moments that framed the country and its presence in the world and how events contributed to the respect our society earned. I have made it an ongoing objective to learn what has truly made our country great over the last two-hundred-plus years, and I have immense admiration for those past and present whose abilities and commitment have benefited Americans while being responsible world leaders.

I did not set out for this to be an anti-Trump book per se; rather, I settled on developing a commentary about specific areas of his abilities or lack thereof and personal characteristics that in a very short time have concerned and even alarmed me. As I thought about what his time as president might mean for our country, I considered the potential damage to our important relationships around the world and to you and me.

What are not contained in this book are opinions about his

moral character, the alleged affairs he had during his marriages, and the multiple lawsuits in play; those will be subjects of other books by other writers. However, I have mentioned the multifaceted allegations surrounding his presidency because though he has not made substantive comments about them, collectively, the allegations form a different comportment of distractions for him personally. Nevertheless, the allegations are disturbing and potentially far-reaching and detrimental to the country.

It is quite impossible for Trump or another person faced with similar circumstances to apply sound thinking to matters important to us all. The many doubts about his suitability as president in the minds of bipartisan members of Congress, political pundits, the media, and world leaders shift the focus to his disjointed tweets. A president is required to have a well-defined focus on issues, historical knowledge, and perspective without which sound decisions would be jeopardized. He instead focuses on himself and creates distractions for Americans and the world.

Do the following words describe Trump as president? Humble. Qualified. Sincere. Ethical. Truthful. Honest. Intelligent. Integrity. Compassionate. Humane. Competent. Empathetic. Civil. I think not, but more to the point, are these not characteristics that should describe someone at the pinnacle of responsibility leading the greatest nation in the world? Many will disagree with what I've written, but as an American who respects our Constitution, I also recognize their right to voice their disagreement because calm and respectable dialogue is important. However, I am confident that there are others, more each day, who will at a minimum understand my objective and determine that my words mirror their concerns.

Every American has the constitutional right of freedom of expression, and exercising that right matters; with issues such as those the country faces today, civil discourse should be encouraged.

Honest and open discussion is what we all deserve. I do not want readers to conclude that I am telling them what to think. On the contrary. I am only providing information to be thought about.

I did not want to defend, support, or criticize any one ideology. Mentions of partisan politics occur because of what appears to be adolescent infighting and lack of cooperation in Congress. Partisan bias is a significant and detrimental daily occurrence, not an avenue to meaningful compromise. The country is tirelessly subjected to Trump's tendency to relentlessly insult Democrats for anything and everything that doesn't go his way when in fact many other factors are in the mix. Our elected officials have engaged in disagreements since our country came to be. Sound debate is welcome, but what we see today goes far beyond debates and disagreements. There are those from both parties elected to serve us who are not disagreeing in constructive ways to find compromise, and having rational and factual discussions with the president has become impossible.

Individuals on both sides of Congress's aisle attempt to understand and carve out paths to cooperation and work with Trump of course, but since his inauguration there is also a decided concentration of effort on the part of senators and representatives to be reelected and retain the Republican majority. This is not unusual of course, but are constituencies being meaningfully served?

President Kennedy said that those who wanted to be successful members of Congress must have "the desire to maintain a reputation for integrity that is stronger than the desire to remain in office." Have some members of the legislative branch of our government lost their way? Are they interested only in staying in Trump's favor and thus have not maintained their integrity? At times, it seems being re-elected outweighs what senators and representatives were sent to Washington to do for us. Elections are of critical importance to all Americans and a change in the majority party in Congress might precipitate a change in Trump's attitude or at least deliver a resounding wake-up call to him. We'll have to wait and see, as Trump says frequently.

Trump's staff and party exhibit an exceedingly dysfunctional approach to our system of government. The troubling part is that the dysfunction began in the 2016 primaries and continued into the election campaign. The dysfunction began to be more obvious after Trump assumed office; the spiral of chaos got into full swing.

Trump changes position from one moment to the next. He regularly misspeaks and then blames others. He makes decisions without understanding situations, and he must obsessively ignore the counsel of his own advisers. Disagreeing with Trump is apparently a career-limiting move. Trump rarely—maybe never—considers the consequences of his actions such as removing security clearances for experienced members of the intelligence community. It's all about him and his personal need for a euphoria-inducing win. Trump wins create unhappiness for others, including the innocent and the country at large.

Some of those who have left the administration may have done so in defense of their principles. Others may have left because they were or are under investigation or because Trump fired them for any number of reasons he justifies in his own mind. In total, those who have departed have one thing in common—they are most probably grateful to escape the chaos. Perhaps deep down, they were justifiably anxious about Trump stumbling into a military conflict, a disastrous long-term economic decline for the country, global alliances further deteriorating, or being associated with the wrath that an unfettered and accidental president might bring down on the US in any number of ways.

I am concerned on many levels. I desperately want to see this degrading national situation turn around. I am a patriot of the highest order. I love this country, its history, and everything it has provided all Americans native born or not. I sincerely appreciate the opportunities I have received as an American for myself, family, friends, colleagues, and those I will never meet. I have traveled the world and have observed what so many others are missing, and I am grateful for the abundance Americans possess. My conversations with people in Kenya, for example, have covered everything from violence and protest during and after elections to the appreciation of PEPFAR[161] in bringing support from the US for HIV/AIDS patients. I respect different viewpoints; while I was a university professor, my discussions with students energized me immensely. I value my experiences, my mentors, and the colleagues I have worked with and the accomplishments we created.

I appreciate how our system of government has met the challenges of the Civil War, economic ruin during the Great Depression, multiple military conflicts from world wars to conflicts in the support of other nations, and an attack on our shores. Through it all, responsible and capable leaders have learned and acted conscientiously, and the country has grown and prospered not by making "deals" but through cooperation, consultation with those more knowledgeable, strategic planning, and compromise.

Those who incite racism and white supremacy include Americans who have benefited from the country's opportunities, growth, and prosperity, but their gratitude is absent and they conveniently forget what our country has provided. Their parochial beliefs have no place in our society, which is constantly at work to overcome such negative viewpoints. Working diligently to influence a positive future for the country through change in thought and improvements in action is what we should be about.

Historically, domestic events that divided the country have been faced head-on not with edicts from a president but with insight and innovation. Some have taken longer than others to resolve because they are difficult and multifaceted. Bigotry and racism still exist, but multiple elements of our society have committed to overcoming these negatives, except for the president. His rhetoric is inflammatory and when told to "tone it down" he makes a conciliatory attempt only to mock the need for this change with language such as "aren't I doing better" at his rallies.

Other countries admire the historic American spirit. We have built relationships with nations around the world based on honesty and integrity and through dialogue and cooperation, not threats. I do not see prospects for growth that reflect these attributes from Trump the man much less Trump the president. He negotiates with himself in strange ways. His operating in less-than-civil ways does not bode well for any sort of positive presidential legacy. This president has already carved out his most lasting descriptors— denial, deflection, division, and distraction.

Many in Congress are trying to defend Trump in some way and at every turn. They are badgering reputable people in the DOJ in hearings to the point of insulting them and accusing them of hiding information. We have seen senators in the majority attack highly qualified and reputable professionals from intelligence agencies for doing their jobs and following established procedures. We have seen committee hearings in both houses of Congress become partisan exercises in contradiction and assaults resulting quite remarkably in 180-degree differences in conclusions.

Even if senators and representatives later admit their previous errored opinions in the most creative forms of mea culpas to save themselves, the impact of their persecution of others will remain. *Saturday Night Live* character Emily Litella, portrayed by Gilda Radner, brushed aside her mistakes with her classic line "Never mind." Those in Congress won't have it that easy. The possibility of recovery in the eyes of the American people will lessen as they have questioned and even interfered with the rigid investigatory process in an extremely partisan manner.

The next steps following the special counsel's findings being delivered to the DOJ are few, but the most alarming scenario, if the House of Representatives deems appropriate, is that prior to Trump's possible impeachment, he might resign as Nixon did. He would not get a pass from obstruction of justice charges, but he could receive a pardon from Pence as Ford gave Nixon. However, there are significant differences between the Nixon situation and what Trump has put the country through for nearly two years. Unlike Ford, Pence has reinforced and supported everything emanating from Trump. I don't believe that makes him presidential material; "Never mind" won't work for him.

I find it extremely hard to believe that Trump has been a model citizen and that there will be no serious ramifications from the long-running investigatory process. Nixon's Watergate cover-up did great harm to the country and its institutions and perhaps most significantly to the importance of trust. What may be lurking in the wings that connect Trump to a variety of charges could have global, not just national, significance. A blind defense of Trump without the benefit of investigation conclusions offers little comfort. There was no expectation that Trump or any other president for that matter would be perfect, but what the country is experiencing is quite a new level of imperfection from the leader of the free world.

As a product of the 1960s, I am reminded of a phrase of that time, "Keep the faith." Unfortunately for many, our president is eroding faith in our democracy and its institutions; his bullish ways do not advance the concepts of leadership, confidence, faith, or success. The country's future is at stake, and ethical people must challenge this dysfunctional presidency. Congress cannot be a bystander. Sane minds, not narcissism, must lead, and truth and integrity must provide the foundation for our future. A critical question is what lasting damage is Trump precipitating for our country? It's a question we cannot fully answer now, but Americans deserve better than to be told to wait and see.

The discussion presented to the public is directed at Trump's issues—from personal lawsuits and criticism of reputable individuals in the DOJ to mysterious interactions with a known enemy of the US, exaggerations of data, false claims, and more. The time spent daily dealing with matters that are not in any sense making America great is regrettable. It's a soap opera of grand proportions that commands our attention, and damage control is at the top of the Trump administration's to-do list each day. Leading the country to a state of ruin that will require years to dismantle and rebuild is unacceptable.

The world is losing respect for the United States because the president has demonstrated he cannot be trusted. Trump is tearing apart long-standing and important global relationships and treaties most likely to the sheer delight of someone like Putin. Others view Trump's manipulative ways as his standard operating procedure, but they can't be admired or accepted as a trusted means of forging productive relationships or demonstrating sound leadership practices. The United States has shown its resilience in facing terrible misfortunes throughout its history. The appalling accident in which the country now finds itself living each day, however, is a tragedy of growing proportions. Watching and waiting while our values and future are further endangered is not a pathway to success.

APPENDIX

TRUMP VOCABULARY PRIMER[162]

atwitter—Nervously concerned. [Twitter is Trump's primary communication tool with minimal credibility but most certainly evidence of his being frequently "all atwitter."]

bias—An inclination of temperament or outlook, especially a personal and sometimes unreasoned judgment. [Trump's inherent view of all others who do not agree with him.]

blame—To hold responsible (they blame me for everything); to place responsibility for (blames it on me). [Either definition is apropos for Trump's practice of blaming others for his lack of credibility and failures.]

brazen—Marked by shameless or disrespectful boldness (e.g., a brazen disregard for the rules). [For Trump, only his rules matter, and his execution of those rules shows little respect for policy, tradition, or institutions.]

bully—A blustering, browbeating person; especially one who is habitually cruel, insulting, or threatening to others who are weaker, smaller, or in some way vulnerable. [A key consideration from this definition is how America and its citizens are vulnerable to Trump's insults and threatening ways.]

character—The complex of mental and ethical traits marking and often individualizing a person, group, or nation (e.g., the character of the American people); moral excellence and firmness (e.g., a man of sound character). [Others' descriptions of Trump do not include any of these attributes.]

complicit—Helping to commit a crime or do wrong in some way. [Be it commentary, collusion, stonewalling, deceptions; many possibilities may arise.]

crooked—Not honest; not straight. [See *dishonest* below.]

disaster—A sudden calamitous event bringing great damage, loss, or destruction. [A word Trump uses frequently and most commonly in reference to his predecessor and Democrats in general, thus far; also, a perfect description of his presidency.]

dishonest—Characterized by lack of truth, honesty, or trustworthiness. [A pointed characterization of others by Trump but interestingly also a description others apply to Trump himself.]

egocentric—Concerned with the individual rather than society. [Trump leads with his self-described expertise and approaches the presidency as only a line on his resume.]

emolument—A return arising from office or employment usually in the form of compensation or perquisites. "No Title of Nobility shall be granted by the United States: And no Person holding any Office of Profit or Trust under them, shall, without the Consent of the Congress, accept of any present, Emolument, Office, or Title, of any kind whatever, from any King, Prince, or foreign State."[1] [Where to begin? Although questions regarding emoluments and Trump have been overtaken by other threatening developments to our country, without the financial disclosure and copies of

---

[1] US Constitution: Article I, Section 9, Clause 8: Emoluments Clause.

separation documents from his businesses, it is difficult to reach conclusions, only suspicions.]

ethical—Conforming to accepted standards of conduct. [This applies to "Never mind."]

fake—A copy of something that is meant to look like the real thing in order to trick people; a person who pretends to have some special knowledge or ability or pretends to be someone else. [Definition 1 describes the president, and definition 2 describes his boasts and persona.]

hoax—To trick into believing or accepting as genuine something false and often preposterous. [A word frequently used by Trump regarding possible untoward occurrences at the time of his election.]

hyperbole—Extravagant exaggeration. [The president's favorite comment on most anything with repeated use of meaningless adjectives and adverbs. He also views hyperbole as a skill and tactic.]

incredible—Too extraordinary and improbable to be believed; making incredible claims. [A word used ad nauseam by the president and his staff most always implying success or expertise in some manner.]

ineptitude—The quality or state of being inept; incompetence. [Trump's belief in himself may be confused with his ability.]

integrity—Firm adherence to a code of especially moral or artistic values. [Perhaps for Trump only a yet-to-be-achieved goal as president.]

liar—A person who tells lies or has a reputation as a liar. [Trump is widely accused of lying in most situations while striving to appear important and knowledgeable or actually accusing someone else of this trait.]

lie—An assertion of something known or believed by the speaker to be untrue with intent to deceive. [Trump and his speechwriters are masters of deception, or so they think.]

loser—A person who is incompetent or unable to succeed. [An accusation aimed at others by Trump who are far from incompetent and have documented success.]

misogynistic—A hatred of women. [Trump has exhibited general hateful and derogatory behavior toward women; he is clearly not comfortable in situations in which powerful and intellectually superior women can challenge him.]

narcissistic—Self-absorbed. [Without question, the Trump-projected image to the world.]

nepotism—Favoritism as in appointment to a job based on kinship. [Trump's adviser selections.]

news—A report of recent events; previously unknown information; something having a specified influence or effect. [No matter which of these definitions Trump may choose to follow, the common ground is fact, not his opinion of the reporting.]

pathological—Being extreme, excessive, or markedly abnormal. [Quite impossible to argue that Trump doesn't have all these characteristics; it is an adequate description of how he is managing his administration.]

patriot—One who loves his or her country and supports its authority and interests. [Trump talks about making America great again but only if others accept everything he says and does without question or criticism. Patriotism is not defined by either of his needs.]

phony—Having no basis in fact. [See *truth* below.]

stratagem—A cleverly contrived trick or scheme for gaining an end. [To be determined ...]

strategy—The science and art of employing the political, economic, psychological, and military forces of a nation or group of nations to afford the maximum support to adopted policies in peace or war. [Breaking this down a bit, Trump has not demonstrated an understanding of science. He adopts crass behavior, not art. He ignores facts, has swiss cheese policies, and provides the distinct possibility of alienating those seeking to improve the country, destroying important global relationships or stumbling into conflicts.]

stupid—Given to unintelligent decisions or acts; acting in an unintelligent or careless manner. [Focusing only on his verbal outbursts, Trump does not provide proof of acting responsibly or smartly.]

truth—The property (as of a statement) of being in accord with fact or reality. [Trump prefers to view his statements as true, but they often do not fulfill the definition of truth.]

unbalanced—Mentally disordered. [Trump does not demonstrate orderliness, only impulsiveness.]

weak—Not able to resist external force or withstand attack; mentally or intellectually deficient; resulting from or indicating lack of judgment or discernment; not able to withstand temptation or persuasion. [The ground is far too fertile here. Pick your favorite descriptor of the president.]

witch hunt—The searching out and deliberate harassment of those (such as political opponents) with unpopular views. [In spite of his endless use of the term, harassment of Trump, no; a search for truth, yes.]

wizard—A wise man; one skilled in magic; a very clever or skillful person. [Trump would agree with all of these definitions and direct them toward himself, but displayed reality at present would easily challenge each of them.]

xenophobia—Fear and hatred of strangers or foreigners or of anything that is strange or foreign. [Trump seems to believe that his past intimidation tactics will lead him to success over all.]

ACKNOWLEDGMENTS

I would not have been able to take on the challenge and responsibility of this effort without the support of many, some of whom encouraged my pursuit of journalism many years ago. These included journalism and history teachers in high school and professors while I was an undergraduate in the Department of Journalism at Indiana University.

From the latter, I learned about media ethics and ethical decision-making, the use of research to guide facts used in writing, and how to apply sound editing techniques that contribute to respect and credibility. I have used this knowledge and these skills throughout my tenure in corporate America and since. I gratefully acknowledge more-recent IU colleagues whom after I returned to my alma mater to teach I had the good fortune to observe and learn from as they influenced my research and writing.

I acknowledge my respect and support of tireless professional journalists who strive to bring insight and truth to the American public in the face of continual accusations of inaccurate and irresponsible reporting. The First Amendment is a treasure of our democracy, and professional and ethical members of the media do not take it lightly or use the freedom it provides in careless ways.

Writing a book requires dedication and discipline particularly when the topic has a seemingly never-ending component of new discoveries, and I acknowledge the influence of my late brother,

T. Michael Elliot, EdD, and his dedication to his career; he was in my thoughts as I journeyed forward. I am grateful to my sister-in-law, Loretta Glaze Elliott, whose reviews, suggestions, and edits helped hone my focus and provided fodder for our sometimes humorous exchanges.

Finally, I acknowledge the support I received from my wife, Catherine Elliott. Though I undoubtedly did not always voice my gratitude to her as I should have, she certainly stood by me and fully appreciated that I considered completing my challenge important. As I spent hours researching components of the content, reading source material, writing, and rewriting, Catherine supported me with her love, and meals at my desk. I'm sure I never thanked her enough, but I do so here and recognize that her commitment to the project was real and appreciated.

REFERENCES

1   Retrieved July 24, 2018, from https://www.vox.com/policy-and policies/2018/7/23/17602278/donald-trump-approval-rating.

2   Retrieved April 5, 2018, from https://www.cnbc.com/2018/4/3/ how-trump-has-weakened-the-worlds-view-of-the-us.

3   Retrieved February 22, 2018, from https://www.cnbc. com/2017/04/26/pope-francis-gives-ted-talk-onleadership-and-solidarity.html.

4   Retrieved June 12, 2018, from http://thehill.com/homenews/ administration/391774-trump-if-i-was-wrong-about-Kim-ill-find-some-kind-of-an-excuse.

5   Article 5 is a provision in the NATO treaty under which an attack on any one member is treated as an attack on the whole alliance, triggering an automatic collective response.

6   Retrieved July 13, 2018, from https://www.washingtonpost. com/world/europe.

7   Retrieved July 16, 2018, from https://www.whitehouse.gov/ briefings-statements/remarks-president-trump-president-putin-russia-federation-joint-press-conference/.

8   Retrieved July 17, 2018, from https://www.nytimes.com/ 2018/07/17/us/politics/trump-putin-russia.html.

9   Martin Luther King Jr., *Stride Toward Freedom* (New York: Harper & Brothers, 1958).

10   Revelation 16:16.

11 Madeline Albright speaking at Voices and Visions series, St. Xavier University, April 11, 2007.

12 R. M. Nixon, retrieved January 15, 2017, from http://www. conservativeforum.org/authquot.asp. (From a 1964 television advertisement supporting Barry Goldwater's bid for the presidency.)

13 H. Levinson, *Ready, Fire, Aim: Avoiding Management by Impulse* (Cambridge, MA: Levinson Institute, 1986).

14 From speech delivered at Trump Tower, New York, on June 16, 2015.

15 Retrieved January 10, 2018, from https://www. usatoday.com/story/news/politics/elections/2016/06/01/ donald-trump-lawsuits-legal- battles.

16 Retrieved September 7, 2017, from http://www.townand countrymag.com/society/politics/a9962852/lawsuits-against-donald-trump.

17 Retrieved June 14, 2018, from https://www.washingtonpost. com/politics/new-york-files-suit-against-president-trump-alleging-his-charity-engaged-in-illegal-conduct/2018/06/14.

18 Retrieved March 3, 2018, from https://www.washington post.com/news/global-opinions/wp/2018/03/12/jeb-bush-was-right-trump-really-is-the-chaos-president.

19 John Adams, "Argument in Defense of the Soldiers in the Boston Massacre Trials," December 1770.

20 Retrieved May 20, 2017, from http://www2.ljworld.com/ news/2017/may/15/opinion-3-us-presidents- and-truth.

21 Trump speech at rally in Albany, NY, December 21, 2016.

22 Retrieved July 18, 2016, from https://www.washingtonpost. com/news/post-politics/wp/2015/11/22/black-activist-punched-at-donald-trump-rally-in-birmingham.

23 Retrieved November 2, 2017, from https://www.cnn.com/2016/02/23/politics/donald-trump-nevada-rally-punch/index.html.

24 Retrieved November 12, 2016, from https://deathofthepressbox.com/2016/11/07/he-made-america-hate-again.

25 Retrieved March 7, 2017, from https://www.sanders.senate.gov/newsroom/press-releases/sanders-statement-on-trump.

26 Twitter, July 29, 2017.

27 Twitter, July 25, 2017.

28 Twitter, August 10, 2017.

29 Twitter, June 18, 2018.

30 A reference to the similarity to the blind faith following of Jim Jones' Peoples Temple movement in Guyana when he and 900 followers died from cyanide injection in November 1978.

31 M. Lerner, "Stop Shaming Trump Supporters," *New York Times*, November 9, 2016.

32 National Public Radio: Fresh Air interview, April 2, 2018.

33 Retrieved February 1, 2017, from https://www.theatlantic.com/politics/archive/2017/01trump-day-one-promises.

34 Retrieved April 7, 2017, from http://www.newsday.com/news/nation/rep-adam-schiff-donald-trump-tweets-need-adult-supervision-1.

35 Statement from Dag Hammarskjold, former United Nations secretary general.

36 Retrieved January 30, 2018, from https://www.brookings.edu/research/after-one-year-in-office-trumps-behind-on-staffing-but-making-steady-progress.

37 Retrieved January 30, 2018, from https//www.brookings.edu/research/why-is-trump-staff-turnover-higher-than-the-5 most-recent presidents.

38 Retrieved July 20, 2017, https://www.nytimes.com/2017/07/19/us/politics/trump-interview-transcript.html.

39   Twitter, December 17, 2016.

40   Twitter, January 6, 2018.

41   Codified in 5 C.F.R. Part 2635 as amended at 81 FR 81641 (effective January 1, 2017).

42   § 2635.101, Subpart A-General Provisions, 5 C.P.R. Part 2635.

43   Retrieved June 1, 2017, from https://www.justice.gove/opa/press-release.

44   (a) Original jurisdiction. The jurisdiction of a Special Counsel shall be established by the Attorney General. The Special Counsel will be provided with a specific factual statement of the matter to be investigated. The jurisdiction of a Special Counsel shall also include the authority to investigate and prosecute federal crimes committed in the course of, and with intent to interfere with, the Special Counsel's investigation, such as perjury, obstruction of justice, destruction of evidence, and intimidation of witnesses; and to conduct appeals arising out of the matter being investigated and/or prosecuted.

45   Retrieved May 12, 2017, from https://www.theatlantic.com/politics/archive/2017/05/exhibit-a-against-donald-trump-his-own-words.

46   From the Greek tragedy *Antigone* by Sophocles, written in or before 441 BC.

47   Retrieved June 15, 2018, from https://www.nytimes.com/2018/06/10/us/politics/trump-turnover.html.

48   Retrieved June 27, 2018, from https://www.cnn.com/2018/06/26/politics/exclusive-pompeo-trump-foreign-policy/index.html.

49   J. R. R. Tolkien. *The Fellowship of the Ring* (United Kingdom: George Allen & Unwin, 1954).

50   L. F. Baum, *The Wonderful World of Oz* (Chicago: George M. Hill, 1900).

51 Retrieved June 12, 2017, from http://www.cnn. com/2017/06/08/politics/paul-ryan-donald-trump-new-to-this/index.html.

52 M. Kalb, *Enemy of the People: Trump's War on the Press* (Washington, DC: Brookings Institution Press, 2018).

53 Twitter June 13, 2018.

54 J. Lott, *The Warm Bucket Brigade: The Story of the American Vice Presidency* (Nashville, TN: Thomas Nelson, 2008).

55 US Code › Title 5 › Part III › Subpart B › Chapter 31 › Subchapter I › § 3110.

56 White House press secretary Sean Spicer, June 6, 2017 press briefing.

57 Twitter, May 8, 2013.

58 Twitter, March 4, 2017.

59 Twitter, March 22, 2018.

60 L. Carroll, *Alice's Adventures in Wonderland* (London: Macmillan, 1865).

61 Retrieved April 25, 2017, from https://apnews.com/c810d7de28 0a47e88848b0ac74690c83/Transcript-of-AP-interview-with-Trump.

62 Retrieved June 20, 2018, from http://www.rasmussen reports.com.

63 *The Wizard of Oz*, Metro-Goldwyn-Mayer, 1939 All rights reserved.

64 Music by Harold Arlen, lyrics by E. Y. Harburg, Metro-Goldwyn-Meyer.

65 D. P. Moynihan and S. R. Weisman, eds., *Daniel Patrick Moynihan: A Portrait in Letters of an American Visionary.* Public Affairs 2010.

66 L. F. Baum, Wallace Denslow, and M. P. Hearn, eds., *The Annotated Wizard of Oz: The Wonderful Wizard of Oz* (W. W. Norton, 2000), 271.

67 *Animal House.* Universal Pictures, 1978.

68 *Dr. Strangelove or How I Learned to Stop Worrying and Love the Bomb*, Columbia Pictures, 1964.

69 Retrieved January 30, 2018, from https://www.quora.com/Why-did-Nixon-say-When-the-President-does-it-that-means-that-it-is-not-illegal.

70 Jean-Baptiste Molière, seventeenth-century French play wright.

71 R. D. Sawyer, *Sun Tzu: Art of War* (Boulder, CO: Westview Press, 1994).

72 Retrieved November 2, 2018, from https://federalregister.gov/d/2017-01798.

73 J. M. Muller, *Adlai Stevenson: A Study in Values* (New York: Harper & Row, 1967).

74 B. Parker and J. Hart, *The Wizard of Id.* Creators Syndicate, 1964.

75 Jean-Baptiste Molière, *Le Misanthrope*, 1666.

76 *Reno v. Flores*, 507 US 292 (1993).

77 Twitter, June 15, 2018.

78 President Donald J. Trump inaugural address, January 20, 2017.

79 W. Shakespeare, a variation on a line spoken by the Queen in Hamlet, "The lady doth protest too much, methinks."

80 Retrieved March 20, 2017, from https://www.msn.com/en-us/news/politics/john-mccain-blasts-trump-for-congratulating-putin-on-winning-sham-election.

81 M. R. Beschloss, *The Crisis Years: Kennedy and Khrushchev 1960–1963* (New York: HarperCollins, 1991).

82 G. Orwell, *Nineteen Eighty-Four* (London: Secker & Warburg, 1949).

83 W. Golding, *Lord of the Flies* (London: Faber & Faber, 1954).

84 Reported White House meeting, July 1, 2017.

85 Retrieved May 6, 2018, from https://www.msn.com/en-us/news/world/nkorea-says-denuclearisation-pledge-not-result-of-us-led-sanctions.

86 Twitter, June 13, 2018.

87 Retrieved June 13, 2018, from https://www.whitehouse.gov/briefings-statements.

88 Retrieved June 1, 2018, from https://www.washingtonpost.com/graphics/politics/trump-claims-database.

89 Retrieved January 24, 2017, from https://www.prsa.org/prsa-2017-chair-jane-dvorak-apr-fellow-prsa-statement-alternative-facts-quoted-politico.

90 With apologies to Walt Kelly and the Pogo comic strip: "We have met the enemy and he is us." First published on Earth Day, April 22, 1970.

91 O. Harari, *Leadership Secrets of Colin Powell* (New York: McGraw-Hill, 2002).

92 Twitter, April 27, 2015.

93 Twitter, May 4, 2015.

94 Twitter, May 24, 2015.

95 Twitter, January 8, 2016.

96 Twitter, January 31, 2016.

97 Twitter, February 9, 2016.

98 Twitter, March 26, 2016.

99 Twitter, March 26, 2016.

100 Twitter, April 8, 2016.

101 Twitter, April 30, 2016.

102 Conservative Political Action Conference speech. Retrieved February 25, 2018, from https://www.vox.com/2018/2/23/17044770/trump-cpac-2018-speech.

103 Retrieved February 23, 2018, from https://www.cnn.com/2018/02/23/politics/trump-latest/index.html.

104 D. J. Trump and T. Schwartz, *The Art of the Deal* (New York: Random House, 1987).

105 *Amadeus*, Orion Pictures.

106 S. Freud, "The Origin and Development of Psychoanalysis," *Amer. J. Psychology* 21, no. 2 (1910): 181–218.

107 Twitter, May 8, 2013.

108 Twitter, March 23, 2016.

109 Twitter, January 23, 2016.

110 Twitter, May 13, 2015.

111 Twitter, September 20, 2015.

112 Twitter, March 22, 2016.

113 Twitter, August 21, 2016.

114 Retrieved May 4, 2018, from http://time.com/5262611/harold-bornstein-donald-trump-doctor-letter.

115 Retrieved May 5, 2018, from https://www.theatlantic.com/health/archive/2018/05/ethics-of-self-assessment.

116 A screening assessment test validated for detecting mild cognitive impairment developed in 1996 by Ziad Nasreddine, MD.

117 Retrieved December 5, 2017, from https://www.nytimes.com/2017/11/30/opinion/psychiatrists-trump.html.

118 American Psychiatric Association. 2Diagnostic & Statistical Manual-V.

119 Product of Wham-O; each bounce of the ball is 92 percent as high as the previous.

120 Retrieved March February 12, 2018, from https://www.economist.com/news/business/21610237-businesses-must-fight-relentless-battle-against-bureaucracy-decluttering-company.

121 D. A. Graham, "Trump's White House Turnover Is Ahead of Schedule," *Atlantic*, January 2, 2018.

122 Executive Order 13770, January 28, 2017, Ethics Commitments by Executive Branch Appointments.

123 Federal Vacancies Reform Act, SEC. 151, Federal Vacancies and Appointments.

124 Dreamworks Classics.

125 Retrieved March 1, 2018, from http://www.newsweek.com/white-house-chief-staff-john-kelly-god-punished-me-donald-trump-department.

126 Retrieved June 12, 2018, from https://thehill.com/homenews/administration/391540-kelly-called-white-house-miserable-place-to-work.

127 Retrieved June 11, 2018, from https://www.nytimes.com/2018/06/10/us/politics/trump-turnover.html.

128 Retrieved May 6, 2018, from https://www.independent.ie/world-news/north-korea-accuses-us-of-misleading-claims-ahead-of-trumpkim-summit-36878323.html.

129 Twitter, June 28, 2018.

130 Retrieved December 12, 2017, from https://www.newyorker.com/magazine/2016/07/25/donald-trumps-ghostwriter-tells-all.

131 M. Ali, "Float like a Butterfly Sting like a Bee." Interview prior to his first fight with heavyweight champion Sonny Liston, 1964.

132 L. J. Peter and R. Hull, *The Peter Principle: Why Things Always Go Wrong* (New York: William Morrow, 1969).

133 US Constitution, Bill of Rights, First Amendment.

134 Report of the Office of the Secretary of Defense Vietnam Task Force. Commissioned by Secretary of Defense Robert McNamara in 1967.

135 *New York Times Co. v. United States*, 403 US 713 (1971), decided June 30, 1971.

136 Retrieved February 12, 2018, from https://www.nytimes.com/1971/07/01/archives/texts-of-the-supreme-court-decision-opinions-and-dissents-in.html.

137 Retrieved March 30, 2017, from https://www.nytimes.com/2017/03/20/opinion/trump-ruins-irony-too.html.

138 W. Lippmann, *Liberty and the News*. (Princeton, NJ: Princeton University Press 1920), 41.

139 J. Rosen, "Public Journalism: First Principles in Public Journalism: Theory and Practice." Dayton, OH: Kettering Foundation Occasional Papers, 1994, 6–7.

140 S. McClellan, *What Happened: Inside the Bush White House and Washington's Culture of Deception* (New York: Public Affairs, 2008), xiv.

141 UN Universal Declaration of Human Rights, 1948.

142 Retrieved March 3, 2018, from http://www.un.org/en/events/pressfreedomday/background.shtml.

143 Retrieved February 26, 2018, from https://cnn.com/2018/01/24/world/pope-condemns-fake-news/index.html.

144 J. McCain, Op-Ed, "Mr. President, stop attacking the press," *Washington Post*, January 16, 2018.

145 "Stupid is as stupid does." *Forrest Gump*, Paramount Pictures, 1994.

146 CNN interview with Anderson Cooper, August 1, 2017.

147 B. Kovach and T. Rosenstiel, *The Elements of Journalism: What Newspeople Should Know and What the Public Should Expect* (New York: Three Rivers Press, 2014).

148 Retrieved June 1, 2017, from https://www.nytimes.com/2017/05/19/us/politics/trump-russia-comey.html.

149 Senator Christopher Dodd (D) Connecticut, served from 1981 to 2011.

150 President Barack Obama, press conference February 9, 2009.

151 Retrieved January 8, 2018, from http://todayinclh.com/?event=journalist-schorr-releases-nixons-enemies-list-discovers-own-name-on-it.

152 Article II, Section I, United States Constitution.

153 Journalist Edward R. Murrow.

154 B. Adler and B. Adler Jr., *The Wit and Wisdom of Edward Kennedy* (New York: Pegasus Books, 2009).

155 Warner/Chappell Music, BMG Rights Management US, LLC, Mose Allison.

156 J. Comey, statement before the United States Senate Committee on Appropriations: Subcommittee on Commerce, Justice, Science and Related Agencies, March 12, 2015.

157 Retrieved January 31, 2018, from http://www.telegraph.co.uk/news/2018/01/14/donald-trump-dangerous-richard-nixon-says-watergate-lawyer-john.

158 Twitter, January 2, 2018.

159 J. Racine, 1*Britannicus*, Narcisse speech, act 4, scene 4.

160 Retrieved July 27, 2017, from https://www.cnn.com/2017/07/26/politics/donald-trump-abe-lincoln/index.html.

161 President's Emergency Plan For AIDS Relief (PEPFAR/Emergency Plan) is a US initiative to address the global HIV/AIDS epidemic and help save the lives of those suffering from the disease primarily in Africa. The program was initiated under President George W. Bush.

162 Root definitions from the Merriam-Webster online dictionary, https://www.merriam-webster.com.